In Our School

Building Community in Elementary Schools

Karen L. Casto, EdD A N D Jennifer R. Audley

ISBN: 978-1-892989-25-3

Library of Congress Control Number: 2007940784

Cover photographs: Peter Wrenn
Interior photographs: Jeff Woodward, Peter Wrenn
Cover and book design: Helen Merena

Northeast Foundation for Children, Inc.
85 Avenue A, Suite 204
P. O. Box 718
Turners Falls, MA 01376-0718

800-360-6332
www.responsiveclassroom.org

12 11 10 09 08   6 5 4 3 2 1

Over the years, we've each had the privilege of working with and learning from teachers, administrators, and other staff in many classrooms and schools. All of those experiences, and in particular our work with educators using the *Responsive Classroom®* approach, have helped us understand the power and importance of building community in schools.

Many people also contributed directly to the making of this book, including the teachers and administrators who responded to our initial survey and an advisory committee that helped us sort through the results and frame the book. That group included Leslie Alexander, Greg Bagley, Ed Barnwell, Marcia Bradley, Andy Dousis, Dick Spindler-Virgin, Tina Valentine, and Chip Wood, all school leaders who have influenced, inspired and generously shared insights with us before and since.

In addition, Paula Denton, Sadie Fischesser, Mary Beth Forton, Cherry McLaughlin, and Michele Sabia reviewed the manuscript at a variety of key stages. Their thoughtful comments and suggestions made this book a better, more complete resource.

Everyone on staff at Northeast Foundation for Children played a role in the publication of *In Our School*. We are particularly grateful to Roxann Kriete for her commitment to schoolwide implementation of the *Responsive Classroom* approach, and to Alice Yang and Helen Merena for their editorial and design contributions.

Finally, we'd like to thank all the people—teachers, administrators, parents—who answered our call for ideas and told us about how they build community in their schools. Their commitment to making schools caring places where children can excel bolstered our enthusiasm for sharing their stories.

Karen Casto would also like to thank—

The extraordinary staff at Penn Valley Elementary School (1995–2005), for creating a strong, caring community of learners for children and adults.

Lynn Majewski, Maryann Fedorko, and Sue DeMeglio for their commitment and dedication to the staff and families at Penn Valley and for their efforts to bring life to a vision.

My parents, Carl and Janet Lynn, for always believing in me and giving me the courage to do what I thought I couldn't.

My husband, Terry, for his endless patience as I worked on this project and his support and love.

Jen Audley would also like to thank—

Susan L. K. Audley, my mother, whose career as a teacher helped me appreciate how rich, challenging, and meaningful a life in education could be.

Martha Goppelt, Tom McHugh, Ted Sizer, and Robin Trainor, teachers of mine who, each in their own way, affirmed my belief that classrooms and schools are deeply interesting and story-filled places.

A Framework for Building Schoolwide Community

A *first grade class waits with nervous anticipation at the front of the gym. As other classes file in, the music teacher begins playing "We're All Together Again," and the first graders start to sing. As students and adults enter, they add their voices, and the volume builds. With teacher assistance, students seat themselves in a horseshoe around the perimeter of the gym. Younger students wave excitedly to their older buddies. Smiles are exchanged.*

The singing continues until all classes have arrived. When the last class is seated, the first graders raise their hands, the school's universal signal for quiet, and the room rapidly comes to attention. Nicole, the first speaker, stands and says confidently, "Welcome to our all-school meeting. Please rise for the Pledge of Allegiance ... "

Gathering for all-school meetings was just one way that Penn Valley Elementary School, where I was principal for nine years, built a strong, caring school community. Holding all-school game days, family literacy nights, and establishing buddy classrooms are a few of the others.

Penn Valley's journey of building schoolwide community began when, after working as a staff to strengthen classroom communities, teachers expressed a desire to extend this sense of community outside their classrooms. They wanted their students to experience a safe, friendly environment not just in classrooms, but throughout the school and throughout the day.

> When an entire school is infused with a sense of community, the effects of community building in classrooms are enhanced.

Children learn best in caring communities where they feel safe and significant. Schools can and should be such communities. Children who feel known and cared for at school are free to focus on learning. They are more able to face challenges with confidence. With the support of a school community, students are motivated to do their best, and teachers and curriculum become even more effective.

Since the classroom is the primary setting for a child's school life, it's incredibly important for children to feel safe and significant there. Good teachers have long understood the value of creating community at the classroom level. However, their efforts can only yield so much, and may even be undermined, if this sense of security is absent in other areas of the school: the hallways, the bus, assemblies, recess, lunch. By contrast, when an entire school is infused with a sense of community, the effects of community building in classrooms are enhanced.

This book is about building schoolwide community. It's made up of stories and examples from schools actively engaged in community-building work. For all of these schools, the journey toward community is a process that has challenged and rewarded as it has unfolded gradually. This journey requires collaboration and commitment from many people. It is hard work. However, when the efforts begin to pay off and a positive sense of community takes hold, the results are often profound.

That was my experience at Penn Valley Elementary School, a medium-sized K–5 public school in Levittown, Pennsylvania. Despite its hardworking teachers and capable students, when I was transferred there from a neighboring middle school in 1995, Penn Valley did not have a good reputation. Schoolwide, morale was poor. Student test scores were low, and many parents were frustrated. Teachers were disheartened because their work didn't seem to be yielding results. There were real problems with discipline. There was little sense of community.

It took nine years of deliberate, step-by-step work for Penn Valley staff, students, and families to build a stronger, more positive school community. During that time, we transformed our approach to teaching and to communication. We established a vision and goals for the school, and we developed schoolwide procedures and routines that reflected them. Then, building on that foundation, we created opportunities for students to work and play in mixed-age groups, developed events that brought the whole school together, and brought parents into the school as true partners.

This process transformed Penn Valley. By the time I retired in 2005, test scores had improved, behavior problems had dropped, and the faculty was strong and proud. Inspiring examples of student work filled the school's hallways; children and adults consistently treated each other with care and respect. In 2003, we were named a National School of Character, and one of our teachers was a finalist for Pennsylvania Teacher of the Year.

What happened at Penn Valley is happening in other elementary schools throughout the United States, with equally powerful results. Schoolwide community looks different at each place, of course, depending on the school's resources, vision, size, and other factors. The goal of this book is to show what schoolwide community looks like at a variety of schools. As you read, you'll find stories from schools in rural, suburban, and urban settings; small schools and large ones; public, private, magnet, and charter schools; schools serving a narrow range of grades (preK–2; 3–5) and a wide range (preK–8); schools that use traditional single grade groupings, and those with multi-age, looping, and bilingual classrooms.

Most of the schools featured in this book use the *Responsive Classroom*® approach to teaching. Developed by teachers and backed by independent research, the *Responsive Classroom* approach is based on the premise that children learn best when they have both academic and social-emotional skills. The approach therefore consists of classroom and schoolwide practices for deliberately helping children build academic and social-emotional competencies. Although using this approach is not a prerequisite for building schoolwide community, for my school and many others in this book, having a unified, philosophically consistent set of practices provides staff and students with a strong foundation for schoolwide work. Our shared experience with *Responsive Classroom* practices such as starting each day with Morning Meeting, involving students in rule creation, and using interactive modeling provided us with an important set of tools for our journey. (To learn more about the *Responsive Classroom* approach, see the Appendix.)

This book is not meant to be a how-to guide. Instead, by showing snapshots from the community-building process as it has unfolded at a variety of elementary schools, it's intended to spark your thinking and to give you ideas. You and your colleagues will need to work together to adapt these ideas for your school. The discussion and planning questions provided at the end of each section are offered as resources to help you work though this process.

Fundamentals of Schoolwide Community

Before you move on to reading the schools' stories, though, I want to share some of what I've learned about the fundamentals of building schoolwide community, based on my own experience at Penn Valley and the experiences of other school leaders I've met along the way.

Qualities of Strong School Communities

Schools that have achieved a positive, enduring sense of community generally share certain broad qualities:

- Staff, students, and their families feel as if they belong at the school and the school belongs to them. Everyone plays a part in making the school feel safe and welcoming for all.

- Adults in the school feel a shared sense of responsibility for children's academic, social, physical, and emotional welfare. Students feel safe and significant wherever they are in the school.

- There are agreed-upon standards for student behavior and learning throughout the school. Adults coordinate their efforts to help students learn to meet those expectations.

- Adults in the school interact with each other in a genuinely caring and respectful manner. Adult relationships within the school community are a model for the friendly, cooperative behavior that's expected of students.

- School staff and families feel they are united in a common enterprise: to support children's optimal learning. School staff and families see themselves as partners, each making vital contributions to children's well-being and success.

Conditions for Building Schoolwide Community

Certain conditions are vital to the growth of community in schools. Although schools often begin work before these conditions are firmly in place, taking steps to create and sustain them is a key to building an enduring schoolwide community.

Strong, Focused Leadership School leaders must provide clear direction, support, and encouragement for community building. They do this by identifying ways to strengthen community in their schools, by setting priorities, by documenting progress, and by celebrating successes. School leaders are role models for students and staff. They set the tone and expectations for the community. While teachers focus on nurturing a particular class's academic and social growth, school leaders must take primary responsibility for building and sustaining the development of the community as a whole.

Commitment from Staff Even the most enthusiastic principal can't build community alone. All adults throughout the building need to see themselves as stakeholders who are making genuine contributions to the change process. The staff must be willing (and in many cases, must learn how) to work together and to coordinate their approach to communicating and interacting with students.

Shared Vision School staff must have a shared vision of what they are trying to achieve—what the school will be like when its sense of community is strong. This vision serves as inspiration and guide for everything that follows. It should be unique, and it may be quite specific.

At Penn Valley, our vision for schoolwide community was inspired by the community-building work that was taking place in classrooms. As classrooms using the *Responsive Classroom* approach became safer and friendlier, and students began thriving academically and socially, we envisioned what it would be like if all areas of our school—including hallways, auditorium, cafeteria, playground, buses, and bathrooms—felt safer and friendlier. For each area, we thought and talked about how people would act and interact, what we would see, and what we would hear. The positive images that emerged became our vision.

The Process of Building Schoolwide Community

The stories in this book describe community-building projects, programs, and events that students participate in directly. As you read, keep in mind that student-centered programs such as these typically require a significant amount of behind-the-scenes work by adults in the school. In each section, you'll learn about how teams of adults approached the process of planning, implementing, and sustaining specific activities at their schools. You'll also find a focused set of discussion and planning questions at the end of each section; these are a resource for your school to use or adapt as you develop your own projects. The discussion and planning questions for the sections are derived from the following guidelines for the process of schoolwide community building:

Assess Take stock of your school's strengths and weaknesses. Spend time observing. How do people act and interact? What do you notice? Listen to how teachers speak to each other, to the children they teach, and to other students. Notice how children treat others: their peers, older and younger children, teachers, and other school staff. Spend time in the cafeteria, on the playground, and in the halls at arrival and dismissal time. Pay attention to what's going well, as well as what could use improvement. Use the information you gather to help you decide what to work on.

Establish schoolwide procedures Small things do matter. For everyday life at school to feel safe, respectful, and friendly, students (and adults) need to know how to do a host of mundane-seeming things. For instance, they need to know how to walk in a crowded hallway, how to sit in a group, how to use an "inside" voice, and how to know when their attention is required. Don't assume that children know what to do—teach these things.

For instance, at Penn Valley, the whole school uses the same visual signal to call for a group's attention: If someone raises a hand, all those who see it immediately raise their hands, stop talking, and look at the person who has given the signal. This technique for quieting a room is taught in every classroom, and used by every teacher many times a day. All the other adults at Penn Valley have learned to use it too, and they have stopped using other ways of calling for attention, such as shushing or yelling. Our commitment to using a universal signal means that in our school, anyone—the principal, a teacher, the custodian, or a first grader—can call a group of any size to order.

Focus Concentrate on improving one area at a time. Don't try to change everything at once, and don't feel obligated to tackle your worst area first. Move slowly and develop a plan before going to work. Try to anticipate problems that might come up before they occur, and allow time for fine-tuning and addressing unforeseen glitches.

Be purposeful Make sure you have a clear, specific reason for undertaking each new initiative before you commit time and resources to it. This will help you choose projects that make sense for your school at the present time and that are aligned with your vision. Once you've committed to a project, having a clear sense of its purpose will guide your planning and will help you monitor your progress.

For instance, when Penn Valley staff learned about the all-school meetings held by other schools using the *Responsive Classroom* approach, we were immediately excited about bringing this community-building tradition to our school. Those all-school meetings adapted elements of daily Morning Meetings held in classrooms for use in regularly occurring gatherings for the whole school. (To learn more about classroom Morning Meetings, see *The Morning Meeting Book* by Roxann Kriete, NEFC, 2002.)

However, we didn't decide to start having all-school meetings at Penn Valley just because other schools were doing it. Before we committed to working together towards this goal, we thought about what the purpose of all-school meetings at Penn Valley would be. We decided that we wanted to create a time when the whole school would share successes and celebrate accomplishments. Gathering for that purpose would enhance students' sense of belonging to a larger school community, would strengthen academic and social connections across grade levels, and would help students get to know and be known by more people in the school.

We also decided on a second purpose: to provide leadership opportunities for students. Each class, including our special needs classes, would be responsible for organizing and running one meeting each year. Every student would experience playing a part in planning and orchestrating a meeting for 350 people.

Deliberating about our purposes not only convinced us that it was worthwhile to commit to a goal of holding all-school meetings in the future—it helped us envision what we wanted them to look and feel like at our school.

Identify and build prerequisite skills
To participate successfully in any activity, adults and children need to be prepared. Teaching or reviewing necessary skills should be a part of your plan.

Choose projects that make sense for your school at the present time and that are aligned with your vision.

For example, with the image of Penn Valley's all-school meetings as joyful, student-led celebrations firmly in mind, we thought about what skills students would need to make it work. It was a pretty long list. For example, just to begin, students had to know how to be a respectful audience and how to enter and exit the gym in an orderly fashion. To sing together, we needed a common repertoire of school songs. And in order to lead all-school meetings, students needed to practice speaking in front of large groups and using our schoolwide signal for attention.

We invested in building these and other prerequisite skills, first in classrooms, and then in progressively larger group gatherings, until finally we were confident that everyone in the school would be able to do them together. As a result, when we started holding student-led all-school meetings, nearly three years after we first started thinking about them, everything went smoothly. Students and staff felt proud and successful.

Start small When you launch a new project, establish a manageable timeline and limit the scope at first if you can. Many of the activities in this book were piloted initially with a few classes and later expanded to include the whole school. You may be able to find other ways to start small. For example, the first year we held all-school meetings at Penn Valley, we only had two, and I led them both. The following year, each class was asked to take responsibility for one meeting during the year, using a scripted format. I provided a model by leading the first one.

Reflect The importance of this step cannot be overestimated. Pause to evaluate each activity, not just after the first time you do it, but periodically. Be sure to celebrate what's going well in addition to thinking about areas you'd like to improve.

> Take time to review and update on a regular basis so that expectations stay consistent and skills remain sharp.

This sort of reflection doesn't have to be formal or time-consuming. At Penn Valley, administrators and teachers sometimes used a regularly scheduled lunch meeting time to discuss things we'd noticed about all-school meeting, such as a bottleneck caused by the way the classes entered, or how much better the singing went when the music teacher played the piano. As a result, we changed the traffic flow in and out of the gym, and we made sure the music teacher was available to play the piano at all of our meetings.

Review As procedures and activities become part of a school's culture, their original purpose may be forgotten. People may slip back into old habits. Changes to programs or schedules may require new procedures. Activities that were once lively and vital may become stale. Take time to review and update on a regular basis so that expectations stay consistent and skills remain sharp. Doing this will also help new staff and students learn about how things are done in your school.

Contents of the Book

The projects and events you'll read about in this book were developed by real schools that are committed to building and strengthening their sense of schoolwide community. In the pages that follow, you'll read about everyday routines, special events, new ways of approaching traditional activities, and many other ways of building, nurturing, and sustaining community in elementary schools. The book is organized this way:

The "Common Knowledge" and "Routines" sections feature stories from schools working on building the foundations of strong, positive community. They focus on topics that apply to daily life at school.

"Gatherings," "Yearly Events," and "Involving Families" describe projects that build on the foundations of common knowledge and schoolwide routines. Gatherings occur regularly and take place during the school day, while yearly events are special occasions. The final section features examples that focus particularly on family participation.

I hope that learning about the schools featured in this book will be as inspiring and exciting for you as it has been for me. Given all that is required in schools today, creating community can easily take a backseat to other issues, and I see the commitment these schools have made and the results of their work as signs of great hope. I hope you will join us, and for that reason, I urge you not to dismiss ideas you read about here because a featured school is very different from yours. It's all too easy to think: "That's nice, but we could never do it. Our school is too … Our students would never … Teachers here don't have … "

Instead, try to make connections. Think about what your school can do, and what you have in common with the schools featured here. Creating community is hard work, but the rewards are many. As you embark on this journey, I wish you courage and joy.

—*Karen L. Casto, EdD*

Common Knowledge

Shared values and expectations help form the basis for community. In a school setting, where community members include students, staff, and students' families, a focus on developing common knowledge can lead to outcomes such as shared understanding of learning goals, a consistent approach to discipline, and all-school traditions that reflect community values. A strong foundation of common knowledge in a school community simplifies communication and serves as a touchstone when decisions have to be made.

However, it's not just any common knowledge that builds community. Common knowledge builds community when students, staff, and families all have a role in deciding "what we believe" and all understand "why we do things this way." All these community members can be involved in envisioning how the school could be, assessing its current strengths and weaknesses, planning next steps, taking action, and reflecting on progress.

In this section you'll read about ways five schools have approached building common knowledge. Their efforts include sharing literature on key themes, helping adults learn to communicate more effectively with children, developing a repertoire of playground games, connecting school staff with classroom life, and creating school-wide rules. Although the projects are different, the schools' stories have some important characteristics in common:

- The projects are undertaken purposefully to address a specific problem or need.

- Schoolwide work builds on established classroom practices.

- Students and staff both play meaningful roles. Parents are involved as much as possible.

- Adults carefully assess whether students have the skills needed for success. When skills are missing, adults teach them to the students.

- Common knowledge evolves as the community's needs change.

The descriptions of schools' efforts in the following pages are not intended to tell the complete story of how to build schoolwide common knowledge. Instead, they are snapshots that show the range of possibilities for work in this area. As you read, think about what common knowledge already exists at your school, and about areas where having more common knowledge might strengthen your school community. Let the descriptions spark ideas for you. When you're ready, use the planning and discussion questions at the end of this section as a resource to guide your school's work in this area.

Common Knowledge

Social Curriculum Book Collections

Each classroom library contains a special set of books on topics of importance to the whole school

PURPOSE

To encourage discussion and understanding of schoolwide themes and common values

W hen Ralph, a kindergartner, visits his second grade buddy's classroom for the first time, one of the book bins in the classroom library catches his eye. "Hey, we have those books in our room, too!" he says. Jamal, the second grade buddy, smiles and pulls out Susan Kuklin's Families, saying, "Want to read this one with me today?"

Every classroom library at Beauvoir contains a copy of *Families* and about ten other books handpicked for their connection to schoolwide themes and issues. A few new books are selected each year, and classrooms all receive their new additions at the same time. Each class reads and discusses each book they receive before adding it to a special section of their classroom library, where the book often becomes a favorite choice for independent reading.

Beauvoir's Social Curriculum Committee chooses the books. Like the other curriculum committees at the school, this group includes a faculty representative from each grade level, an administrator, and several special areas teachers (called "resource teachers" at Beauvoir). The committee's role is to support and improve ways the school helps children develop social skills. The group has developed benchmarks and standards, discussed behavioral guidelines, and brainstormed ways to promote schoolwide understanding of the Beauvoir Life Rules: Be respectful, Be responsible, Be kind, and Be honest. They spend part of each of their meetings considering new selections for the classroom libraries.

Holly Joyner, guidance director and co-chair of the committee, says that sometimes members recommend specific books, or the committee identifies a theme and looks for books that relate to it. *Families* was added as a result of a recent effort to diversify the ways families are represented in books read at Beauvoir. "We were looking for books that showed families all of our students could relate to, including families with divorced parents, with single parents, and families headed by grandparents. We also wanted books that could be read in age-appropriate ways with children ranging from pre-K to third grade."

Some of the social curriculum books are read aloud in conjunction with school-wide events. For example, readings of Page McBrier's *Beatrice's Goat* kick off the school's annual coin collection project for Heifer International®.

BENEFITS

"The social curriculum books help us unify our approach to reinforcing social skill learning," says Ms. Joyner, explaining that having all classes read the new books simultaneously creates common ground for discussions about social curriculum issues. Children in different classes talk to each other about the books, and when buddy classes visit one another they see that books that are special in one classroom are special in many classrooms. This sends a powerful, consistent message about what's important in this particular school culture.

While the new books that are added to the collection may get the children's initial attention, the old favorites play an important role as well. Ms. Joyner reports that children enjoy rereading the social curriculum books from year to year, and that as they age, their understanding of the issues presented in them deepens.

The books play a role in helping students develop their reading skills as well. While reading and taking in content about social issues, they are practicing decoding, using context clues, increasing their reading fluency, and building vocabulary. Discussions about the books also help children learn about character development, plot, and other literary elements.

KEYS TO SUCCESS

Adequate funding is provided At Beauvoir, funding for the classrooms' social book collections is included in the school's general budget. While dependable financial support from the administration frees Beauvoir staff to focus on selecting the books and supporting their use in classrooms, a program such as this one could also be supported by a parent organization or funded by grants.

Book choices match school values and student needs The care the Social Curriculum Committee invests in researching and selecting books for this program results in selections that match the needs of Beauvoir students. This school community already had a strong sense of common values when the program began, and the committee builds on this foundation when selecting books. They strive to address a range of topics and to choose books that will be appropriate and appealing for pre-K to third grade students.

Teachers support the project Beauvoir teachers' enthusiasm for this program helps it succeed. When new books come to their classrooms, they make it a special event by reading the book and discussing it with the children before officially placing it in the classroom library.

Tacky the Penguin BY HELEN LESTER Concepts highlighted include individuality and "same and different."

Beatrice's Goat BY PAGE McBRIER Used to begin Beauvoir's schoolwide collection for Heifer International® each year.

Boxes for Katje BY CANDACE FLEMING Used to promote community service, global awareness, and kindness.

Families BY SUSAN KUKLIN Acknowledges many different kinds of families.

It's Back to School We Go: First Day Stories from around the World BY ELLEN JACKSON Concepts highlighted include "same and different," cultural perspectives and understanding, and respect.

A Walk in the Rain with a Brain BY EDWARD M. HALLOWELL Explains that there are many different types of thinkers and many different ways of being smart.

Some of the books in Beauvoir's social curriculum book collections

Lunchtime
Teacher Language

Staff trainings lead to a calmer,
more orderly cafeteria

PURPOSE

To spread the
use of effective
communication
techniques from
classrooms into
common spaces

T*he lunchroom is buzzing with dozens of conversations when Ms. Brunton, one of several lunch teachers on duty, silently raises her hand, the school-wide signal for quiet attention. Children at several tables see the signal, stop talking, and raise their hands, too. Their tablemates and neighbors copy them, and in less than a minute, the entire room is quiet and all eyes are on Ms. Brunton, who then lowers her hand and calmly begins giving directions.*

A few years ago, lunchtime at Kensington Avenue was often noisy and chaotic, a situation that was intensified by a basement setting with a challenging layout and a lunch staff with little formal training in supervision. Since problems that started in the lunchroom often carried into the afternoon, school leaders at Kensington decided to prioritize making lunchtime a more peaceful, pleasant experience.

A group of teachers, staff, and parents met and decided to offer professional development to the lunch staff, or "lunch teachers," as they're called at Kensington. The goal was to help the lunch teachers use the same communication techniques that teachers were using successfully with students in their classrooms. The group reasoned that because teacher language can have a huge impact on children's behavior, such consistency should help students carry calm and respectful classroom behavior into the lunchroom. (To learn more about the approach to teacher language used at Kensington Avenue, see *The Power of Our Words* by Paula Denton, NEFC, 2007.)

The project began with a workshop early in the school year. Lunch teachers were asked to come to school early one day for the session and were compensated at their regular wage for attending. Tina Valentine, then Kensington's head teacher,

---

Kensington Avenue School, Springfield, Massachusetts
urban; public ▪ K–5 ▪ 337 students ▪ 16 classrooms ▪ 87% of students receive free or reduced-price lunch

showed them how to:

- Use the all-school signal for quiet. The lunch teachers practiced using the signal without adding other verbal directions (such as shushing or talking), hand signals (such as finger pointing), or facial expressions, and then waiting for quiet.

- Use positive language to remind children about behavioral expectations ("Show me what you should be doing right now") or to reinforce good behavior ("I see that you're keeping your hands to yourself"). The lunch teachers practiced using this kind of language together.

- Keep directions to students clear and simple—For example, saying, "Stop. The trays go on the stack here," instead of "You are not supposed to put your tray there. We have talked about safe stacking of trays, and the way you put your tray is not safe. Please remove your tray and stack it the way it is supposed to be stacked."

After the workshop, Ms. Valentine modeled using the techniques in the lunchroom and observed the lunch teachers as they practiced. After a few weeks, she met with the lunch teachers to debrief about how things were going and problem solve. Then, throughout the year, she provided one-on-one coaching and occasional group refreshers on an as-needed basis.

In the years since, a similar workshop has been offered to Kensington's lunch teachers at the beginning of each year. Returning and new staff are invited to attend, and Ms. Valentine says that even veteran lunch teachers appreciate the review, explaining "It's good to get it in your head again after the summer. You can't hear this stuff too many times." After the first year, the more experienced lunch teachers began mentoring newcomers, doing some of the modeling and coaching that Ms. Valentine provided during the first year.

BENEFITS

The lunchtime environment at Kensington improved dramatically after the school began working with the lunch teachers this way. Lunch became a safer and more successful place for children, so fewer behavioral issues arose, and the transition into the afternoon in the classroom went more smoothly.

Building on the success of the lunch teacher trainings, the school began offering similar workshops and coaching, with some modifications, to office and custodial staff. Now, Principal Margaret Thompson notes, "You just don't hear adults raise their voices at children here."

This process also helped the lunch teachers feel more respected and connected to the school community. They credit the workshops with helping them feel more comfortable with the children, as well as with being able to communicate with them

> "It's really important for the staff to feel supported as they learn and try new things."

more effectively. Furthermore, because debriefing and problem solving sessions are included in the learning process, the lunch teachers have been able to contribute their observations and insights to the school's ongoing efforts to improve children's social and emotional welfare.

KEYS TO SUCCESS

Communication techniques are consistent schoolwide The communication techniques learned by the lunch teachers at Kensington mirror those already being used in classrooms throughout the school. For instance, because students had already learned how to respond to the signal for quiet, it was easy for the lunch teachers to begin using the signal in the cafeteria. Furthermore, having the same expectations and ways of communicating the same as other teachers reinforced the lunch teachers' authority.

Coordinator works well with adult learners When this effort started at Kensington, having a highly skilled coordinator was crucial. Already a master at using the communication techniques with children, Tina Valentine created a learning experience for adult staff that was focused, positive, and effective. "The person who does the training has to be someone people feel comfortable with," says Ms. Valentine. "It's really important for the staff to feel supported as they learn and try new things."

Follow-up support is offered The school recognized that offering the initial workshop to lunch staff was just a start. By offering follow-up coaching and an annual refresher course, Kensington helped the lunch teachers learn to apply new skills successfully. This follow-through also sent the message that the school's commitment to improving lunch behavior was genuine, and that staff played a valuable role in that process.

PURPOSE

To make recess
a fun, safe, and
peaceful time
for all

Teaching Recess

Starting the year with shared expectations
and a repertoire of games for the playground

I t's the first day of school, and Ms. Leib is teaching her class of first and second graders the "Freeze!" signal, an important safety procedure for recess. As part of the lesson, the children have just watched three of their classmates demonstrate how to respond to this command. When Ms. Leib asks what they notice, the children have many observations: "They stopped moving right away ... They stopped talking ... They made sure they were looking at you when they froze."

Ms. Leib acknowledges each comment and then asks, "How could using this signal help us stay safe and have fun on the playground?"

A scene like this one takes place on the first day of school in every classroom at Penn Valley. It's the beginning of a sequence of events that help get recess off to a good start each year by establishing schoolwide expectations for safe play and by building a common repertoire of games.

The process, which unfolds over several days at the beginning of school, starts before children go outside for the first time. Each class discusses ways to make outdoor time safe and fun and practices responding to commands that will be used during recess, such as "freezing" for an announcement or "circling up," so an adult can give directions to the whole group.

Then, for the first few days of school, teachers and administrators join students and recess aides on the playground during recess. The adults lead structured games that give students an opportunity to practice the skills of safe play. During this time, children practice circling up, learn the boundaries of the play area, and become familiar with what "safe tagging" feels like (a firm but gentle touch on the back or the arm). They also

Penn Valley Elementary School, Levittown, Pennsylvania
suburban; public ■ K–5 ■ 310 students ■ 18 classrooms ■ 25% of students receive free or reduced-price lunch ■ multi-age classrooms for 1st and 2nd grade ■ 5 self-contained special education classrooms

learn to resolve disputes by using the schoolwide "tagger's choice" rule, which says that the person doing the tagging determines whether a tag counts.

Finally, on the first Friday of the school year, Game Day familiarizes students and staff with a common repertoire of playground games. There are two sessions, one for primary and one for upper grades. During their session, each class rotates through six to eight stations, learning a new playground game at each fifteen minute stop. Teachers run the stations; classroom and recess aides travel and learn the games with the students. A bell rings when it's time for students to move to the next station. Along with age-appropriate cooperative games, there's a station where proper use of playground equipment such as swings is demonstrated, and, for students in the upper grades, a review of rules for popular games such as kickball and four-on-four soccer. At the end of Game Day, every teacher and the recess aides receive written directions for playing all the games students have learned.

From this point on, with a clear understanding of expectations for recess behavior and a repertoire of games to draw on, Penn Valley students begin choosing how to spend their recess time. Some organize their own games, while others join in activities led by one of the recess aides. Equipment for the period is kept on a cart outfitted with balls, jump ropes, bases, chalk, and other age-appropriate materials.

For the next few weeks, the children continue to learn new games and to practice fair play in gym class, where the first curriculum unit focuses on playground games. Physical education teacher Brian Doron keeps the recess aides updated on what he has been teaching. He also comes to recess when his schedule permits.

BENEFITS

Penn Valley has introduced recess this way for almost ten years, and the staff has seen lasting positive effects, including fewer conflicts on the playground and a notable shift, particularly in the upper grades, from exclusionary to inclusive games. Teachers report that students often choose to play the games they learned at Game Day. There's less quarreling over rules and more time for fun.

Having consistent expectations for recess behavior from grade to grade has made this part of the day much more manageable for staff and students. The basic signals and procedures carry over from year to year, so with practice and focused review at the beginning of the year, children internalize them. Safe, inclusive behavior on the playground has become a part of the school's culture.

The process of getting recess off to a strong start involves the whole school in a unified effort that benefits everyone by building common understanding, common language and common expectations. Students, teachers, administrators, and aides all contribute to creating a positive atmosphere on the playground, and all take pride in the results.

Staff are involved in every aspect Karen Casto, who was principal of Penn Valley when the school began using this approach to teaching recess, stresses the importance of getting buy-in from staff. "Have a conversation about recess in which everyone has a chance to talk about what it's like now, how they'd like it to be, and what's needed to make it happen. Help them see that by setting common expectations and working together to create a recess that is peaceful and fun, you will reduce the number of playground conflicts coming into the classroom and disturbing learning." Penn Valley also asks staff members to fill out an evaluative survey after each Game Day; this feedback influences planning for the future.

Parents understand the purpose of recess changes Dr. Casto also suggests "communicating with parents about what you are doing and why. We had some complaints early on that the children weren't having 'fun' at recess anymore (because they weren't being allowed to run around and be wild). We realized that we needed to do a better job of explaining the purpose behind teaching recess." After explaining at PTO meetings and in the school newsletter that the new, more structured recess was a proactive strategy to help make recess a fun, safe and conflict-free time, Dr. Casto found that parents became more supportive.

A coordinator organizes and oversees Instructional support teacher Lynn Majewski originally organized the teaching of recess at Penn Valley; more recently instructional support teacher Sue DeMeglio and physical education teacher Brian Doron have shared this responsibility. In the first years, there was quite a bit of preparation involved, including scheduling Game Day, choosing games and teaching them to teachers and aides, typing up directions, marking the field, and gathering equipment. Since then, some elements have become more routine (for instance, many teachers teach the same game each year), but pulling it all together continues to require considerable oversight, careful planning, and help from volunteers.

PURPOSE

To provide
opportunities
for staff members
to participate in
classroom life

Staff Buddies for Classrooms

Staff members join a classroom
for events throughout the year

Second grade teacher Kristin Eisenhardt pops her head out her classroom door as Laura Page walks past and asks, "Do you have time to come in and see what the class is doing right now?"

When Ms. Page enters, the students greet her enthusiastically, and she spends a few minutes moving comfortably from table to table, chatting with each group about their work before heading back to her office. Later in the week she'll return to read from the book she's been sharing with this, her buddy class.

Each of the nineteen classes at Beauvoir is paired with a staff member whose work takes place mostly outside the school's classrooms. These adults join their buddy classes throughout the year for activities such as reading books, attending Morning Meetings, and going on field trips. This voluntary program connects staff members with what's happening in classrooms, and it helps children get to know the adults who work at the school.

Holly Joyner, guidance director at Beauvoir, coordinates the program. Each year, after finding out which of the current classroom buddies want to continue, she recruits new volunteers to fill the spaces that remain. When matching buddies with classroom teachers she considers their requests and schedule constraints, as well as other compatibility issues. She notes that "just because a person works in a school doesn't mean that they feel comfortable with kids, or being in a classroom," so it's important to match staff buddies with teachers who can give them the amount of guidance they need.

Staff buddies and the classroom teacher they're matched with decide how they'll work together on their own. Arrangements vary considerably. For instance, Ms. Joyner eats lunch

Beauvoir, The National Cathedral Elementary School, Washington, DC
urban; independent ▪ pre-K–3 ▪ 380 students ▪ 19 classrooms

with her first grade buddy class on Fridays and sometimes teaches greetings and activities during Morning Meeting. Other staff buddies come to the classroom to greet children as they arrive in the morning, or sit with their buddy class at all-school meetings.

Ms. Joyner says that this program has strengthened relationships within the school. She has noticed that children now know more adults' names, and that they enjoy seeing their new adult friends in and outside of the classroom. Knowing more staff members increases the children's sense that people throughout the building care about them and will look out for them. Plus, she adds, "The staff buddies say they love participating in classroom life. This program helps them gain a deeper appreciation for the primary work of the school, and it helps them see how their work contributes to the community."

In some cases, staff buddies play a significant role in classrooms. For instance, second grade teacher Kristen Eisenhardt says her class's buddy, assistant to the division directors Laura Page, "is totally a part of our class. The kids love her, and because she is here regularly, she really knows them and is able to fit right in."

KEYS TO SUCCESS

Supportive environment Beauvoir's school culture is well-suited to a staff buddy program. The school's Beauvoir Buddies program has been pairing up children from different grades for more than twenty years, and the idea of connecting non-teaching staff with classrooms was proposed by a group of staff members. The program thrives because it exists in a school culture where the time staff members spend with their buddy classes is seen as valuable and a contribution to the school community.

Voluntary participation It's also proven important that staff choose whether to participate. Initially, every Beauvoir staff member was assigned to a classroom, but school leaders quickly realized that the program would work better if it was voluntary. As Holly Joyner explains, "Now that people choose to participate, everyone who does it is excited to be involved." Finding a buddy for every classroom has never been a problem: many buddies choose to continue from year to year, and it has not been difficult to find volunteers for the remaining openings.

Skillful coordination Finally, Ms. Joyner's behind-the-scenes work is vital to keeping this program running smoothly. Although the staff buddies and classroom teachers do most of their planning and scheduling independently, Ms. Joyner's skill at making successful pairings sets the stage for their success. She also promotes the program by talking about it at staff meetings, and she supports teacher/buddy planning with a weekly email message that asks "Have you seen your buddies lately?" and suggests times to visit and things to do.

Creating Schoolwide Rules

Students take center stage in setting consistent expectations throughout the school

A *handsome poster in the front hallway of Sheffield Elementary School states four rules that govern student and adult behavior throughout the school:*

Enjoy!
Respect everyone and everything.
Be helpful and responsible.
Take care of school property and classrooms.

Poetic in their simplicity and brevity, these four rules encompass all the expectations for behavior everywhere in the school. They were created by the school's students as one element of a larger, long-term school climate improvement process.

The Sheffield schoolwide rules were created in response to a challenge familiar to many educators: how to employ a consistent approach to discipline throughout the school, not only in classrooms, but in common areas such as the playground, lunchroom, and hallways as well. The groundwork for developing schoolwide rules was laid over many preceding months, beginning with a lengthy and ultimately successful effort to develop consensus among the school's adult community about discipline practices, as well as common guidelines for responding to behavior problems.

Also, classroom rules were in place before work on schoolwide rules began. Each year at Sheffield, students and teachers create classroom rules during the first weeks of school—typically these are three to five broadly stated guidelines about taking care of themselves, each other, and classroom materials and spaces. When they created their schoolwide rules, Sheffield extended this process beyond the classroom, using a multi-step "convention" structure that gave students a central role:

Sheffield Elementary School, Turners Falls, Massachusetts
rural town; public ▪ grades 3–6 ▪ 270 students ▪ 11 classrooms ▪ 56% of students receive free or reduced-price lunch

Grade-level conventions Each of the school's classes chose two delegates to represent them at a grade-level convention. The job of the delegates—about seven per grade—was to discuss all the classroom rules for their grade and synthesize them into three to five rules. One grade's delegates voted rule-by-rule for inclusion or exclusion; another's grouped similar rules to more easily decide among them. When these meetings were complete, there were four sets of rules, one set for each of the grades in the school.

Final convention Each grade's group of delegates selected two members to represent their grade at the final convention. One day in late September, Sheffield's principal and guidance counselor convened these eight students in a conference room and charged them with the task of transforming four sets of grade-level rules (a total of approximately sixteen rules) into a handful that could be applied throughout the school. The students took their task quite seriously and deliberated for an hour and a half before arriving at their final four schoolwide rules.

Soon after the final convention, the rules were adopted formally at a rule-ratification ceremony attended by the whole school community, including students, teachers, other staff, and parents, along with school district officials, local government and town leaders, and members of the local media. The eight final convention delegates explained and role-played each of the four rules before the list was affirmed by voice vote and a stirring standing ovation. This marked the beginning of the next phase of the journey: reflecting on and practicing living by the rules.

This part of the work is ongoing. It's what makes the rules "more than just a sign on the wall," says principal Chip Wood, and what keeps them alive year after year, even for students who were not present when the rules were created. The schoolwide rules are included in the handbook each family receives at the beginning of the year, and are reviewed and discussed at Sheffield's first all-school meeting each year. They are reinforced during the first weeks of school as children are oriented to common areas such as hallways, cafeteria, and playground. Teachers also enhance the annual classroom rule making process by having students compare classroom and schoolwide rules. Finally, students who exemplify the schoolwide rules in specific ways in their behavior are commended through positive notes sent home.

BENEFITS

Creating schoolwide rules was a significant landmark in Sheffield's ongoing work on improving school climate, says Mr. Wood. The rules, displayed not only at the school's entrance but in every classroom and common space as well, offer a tangible signal to students that the same high standards for conduct in their classroom apply in every classroom and every school space, from the art room to the playground to the lunchroom to the bathroom to the bus.

Having a set of schoolwide rules also signals to the adults at school that high expectations apply across the board. And it gives all adults a consistent way to talk with students about behavior. When a child goes off track, any adult can refer to the school rules—saying, for example, "Anita, what do our school rules say about how to talk to each other?"

Finally, the rule creation process offered many academic tie-ins. For example, the experience gave students firsthand experience with one way that democratic decision-making can be structured. Some classes learned that the convention process Sheffield used resembled that used to create the U.S. Constitution. And in distilling many rules down to a few, delegates discussed and arrived at fairly nuanced understandings of words such as "respect" and "responsible," which appeared in many classroom rules.

KEYS TO SUCCESS

Mr. Wood emphasizes that to be effective, any effort to create schoolwide rules must be part of a comprehensive, schoolwide approach to discipline that is supported by all staff. At Sheffield, this includes:

Classroom rule creation and rule teaching Every fall, every teacher at Sheffield involves students in creating rules for their own classrooms. The children begin by articulating their hopes for the year, and then, with the teacher's guidance, create rules that will foster an environment in which each class member can achieve his or her hopes. Teachers model and give children opportunities to practice translating these rules into action in various everyday situations, from writer's workshop to packing up at the end of the day. This classroom-level work hones children's appreciation for respecting rules, which helps ensure that both classroom and schoolwide rules have power and meaning.

Clear steps for responding to rule breaking Knowing that even with the best proactive teaching all children will make mistakes sometimes, Sheffield has a set of written, clear steps for all staff to use consistently in handling problems. The steps progress from a reminder about expected behavior, to a time-out and other measures to help children regain control (such as taking a break in another teacher's classroom), to suspension for serious misconduct. When all adults use these steps consistently, says Mr. Wood, children gain a greater sense of security and are more likely to maintain respectful, caring behavior throughout the school.

Involvement of parents Parents are an important part of Sheffield's discipline approach. For example, the steps for responding to misbehavior were based not only on discussions among staff, but also on a survey of all parents (and students). The steps are included in the parent handbook. Similarly, when the schoolwide rules were created, copies were sent home to parents. Mr. Wood also emphasizes the importance of involving parents in ongoing classroom and school activity related to discipline, for instance by sending frequent letters home, inviting parents to share their hopes and concerns for their child, and using back-to-school nights and parent conferences to talk about the school's discipline approach.

Sharing Classroom Rules

A yearly tradition compares classroom rules with established schoolwide rules

At Deer Isle-Stonington Elementary School (DISES) in Deer Isle, Maine, students and teachers in each classroom create rules together at the beginning of the year. Each set of classroom rules includes three to five positive statements everyone agrees to try to live by, such as "Stay safe," "Be kind," and "Take care of your environment." Students are expected to follow their rules in every area of the school, including classrooms, cafeteria, playground, gym, art, and music rooms.

Each October, the school holds a Constitutional Convention, at which representatives from all eighteen classrooms gather to share their rules with each other. The meeting takes place in the library and is presided over by the principal, assistant principal, and the librarian. The principal reads the school constitution, a document modeled on the Preamble to the U.S. Constitution that includes the schoolwide rules developed at DISES some years ago. Each student delegate is asked to affirm that his or her classroom rules are compatible with the schoolwide rules.

Next, the students take turns standing to read their class's rules aloud before presenting them to the administrators, and then each signs the School Constitution. After the meeting, the School Constitution, all the classroom rules, and a photo of the delegates are posted on a hallway bulletin board for the whole school to see.

Teacher Paula Greatorex says that teachers and students always notice many similarities among the rules across the grades, and that this reinforces the fact that the school's expectations for behavior and its approach to discipline are consistent for students of all ages. This activity also spotlights the values that all members of the DISES community share, including their commitment to making their school a safe, friendly place.

Deer Isle-Stonington Elementary School, Deer Isle, Maine
rural; public ▪ K–8 ▪ 250 students ▪ 18 classrooms ▪ consolidated island school

Common
Knowledge

37

Discussion and Planning Questions

These questions are intended for use by groups such as school leadership teams, parent-teacher partnerships, and cross-grade committees who have chosen to work together on building schoolwide community.

The suggestions on these pages are intended to help guide your group through the process of considering, planning, and implementing initiatives to build common knowledge at your school.

Before choosing a specific focus:

Assess Consider the common knowledge that already exists at your school.

- What values and expectations do students, teachers, staff, and parents share? How do you know?

- What could you build on?

- What might be a good place to start?

Be purposeful Make sure you can explain what the school community hopes to gain from working on common knowledge.

- What results do you hope to see?

- Who will benefit? How?

Focus Define a specific project that fits your purpose and has realistic, measurable goals that mesh with other plans for school improvement.

Then, as you plan, consider how different members of the school community will be included in achieving those goals.

- How will students, staff, and others be involved in planning, participating, and reflecting?

Once you have selected a project:

Start small Try to divide the project into manageable parts or phases.

- Could you do a pilot version before taking it schoolwide?

- What else could you do to help ensure success?

Introduce the project Make sure everyone who will be involved understands the project and its goals.

- How will the project be introduced to adult participants?

- How will it be introduced to students?

- How will students' families learn about it?

- Who else needs an introduction and how will they get it?

Prepare If necessary, teach and practice prerequisite skills in classroom or smaller groups.

- For this to succeed, what do people need to know how to do?

- When and how will they be prepared?

Afterwards:

Evaluate and celebrate Take time to stop and reflect on how things are going. Think about and celebrate successes as well as things that need to be improved.

- Is it working the way you expected?

- Have there been any surprises?

- What has been successful?

- What could make this go better?

Update Review your purpose and goals periodically. Consider the goals you had for doing a particular project, and for working on common knowledge in general.

- Has your purpose changed?

- Is it time to set different goals?

Routines

Routines are ways of doing everyday tasks that are practiced until they become habit. In school, routines help create a familiar, safe environment so that children and adults can focus their energies on learning. Just as academic routines are a basic element of successful teaching and learning, schoolwide routines lay the groundwork for success in many areas of school life.

For instance, teaching students how to walk quietly and respectfully through the halls at the beginning of the year establishes expectations that help keep hallways calm. The details of such routines vary from school to school—students might be allowed to wave silently to friends as they pass, or they might be required to pause at hallway intersections for an adult's direction. The common denominator is that after being given time to practice, everyone in the community knows and is expected to follow the routine.

Developing successful routines requires students and staff to "live their rules" by translating them into actions. For example, thinking together about what it might look and sound like to live by a rule such as "Stay safe and respectful" in the lunchroom or on the playground is typically the first step in building schoolwide routines for those places.

Routines are most likely to succeed if all members of a school community are involved in their creation. When they are developed collaboratively and are in harmony with the values of a school, routines can strengthen its sense of community.

In this section, you'll see examples of routines for shared spaces and times at six schools. By establishing a welcoming and calm tone as children arrive for school, creating a calm and respectful atmosphere in the cafeteria, making dismissal a smooth, positive experience, and striving for "more good days on the bus for everyone," these schools make a positive impact on the learning environment for their students. Some of the key characteristics shared by their stories are:

- Routines are built on skills students have already learned and practiced in their classrooms.

- Routines are modeled, taught, practiced, and reinforced over time.

- When appropriate, input from staff members and students is solicited, considered, and incorporated into the design of the routines.

- Families and others in the extended school community know about and respect schoolwide routines.

- Routines are reviewed and revisited in school at the beginning of each year.

As you read this section, think about shared spaces or times in your school. Use the featured schools' stories for inspiration, considering ways that your situation is similar to and different from theirs. Then, when you are ready, turn to the discussion and planning questions at the end of the section and begin exploring ways routines might be used to build community at your school.

SECTION TWO
Routines

PURPOSE

To establish
a welcoming,
calm tone as
children enter
the school
building

Arrival Time

Clear expectations and warm welcomes
keep arrival time calm and safe

As soon as she hears children entering the building at the beginning of the school day, Linda Stephenson, the guidance counselor at Dame School, steps out of her office and stands by her door. As the children head down the long corridors that lead to their classrooms, they pass Linda and several other adults, who each smile and greet them: "Hello, Kyle! Good morning, Evie!"

Some children respond to the adults' greetings with a cheerful "Good morning!" Others return a quiet nod, rush over for a quick hug, or share a brief conversation. Then, within a few minutes, the flow of students through the hallways becomes a trickle, and the classroom day begins.

The hallways at Dame School used to look different at arrival time. Children would enter the building haphazardly, talk loudly, and run down the halls. This unruly and potentially unsafe transition from playground to classroom frustrated and worried the staff. "You could just feel the tension in this place, from the start of the day to the end," says first grade teacher Dawn Morris. School leaders addressed the problem with a two-pronged approach: by teaching students clear expectations for hallway behavior, and by asking adults throughout the school to be greeters in the hallways during morning arrival time.

The Dame Leadership Team, which consists of administrators, teachers, support staff, and parents, led this effort. They arrived at their two-pronged solution by first articulating a clear goal: to achieve a pleasant atmosphere by helping children maintain self-control as they traveled through the long hallways. And, in thinking of ways

---

Dame School, Concord, New Hampshire
suburban; public ■ preK–2 ■ 305 students ■ 17 classrooms ■ 46% of students receive free or reduced-price lunch
■ building also houses a comprehensive neighborhood family resource center

Since the expectations for hallway behavior were the same for everyone in the school, the children received consistent feedback about what they were doing well from many different adults.

to achieve this, they focused on proactive, positive strategies rather than reactive, punitive ones. Here's how the school worked on each aspect of the solution.

Teaching hallway behavior

The first step was teaching the children how safe, friendly hallway behavior looks, feels, and sounds. The adults began by agreeing among themselves what constituted such behavior, from walking at a safe speed to looking where you're going. Then the teachers discussed this with their students and modeled the desired behaviors. For example, Ms. Morris asked the children in her class to observe her as she walked down the hallway, and then afterwards asked them to share what they noticed about her "calm, safe walking." The children noticed things like "You went straight," "You kept your hands at your sides," "You walked slowly the whole time." Ms. Morris guided them to name further details, for example by asking, "Who noticed what I did with my eyes?" so students would identify "look where you're going" as a behavior.

Then, once many qualities of safe walking had been named, the children began to practice, first by having a few at a time model while others observed, and then together as a class. For the next few weeks, all teachers watched carefully for instances of hallway behavior that met expectations. They reinforced the children's learning by pointing out specifically what they were doing well, using comments such as "I noticed that you kept your hands at your sides the whole way to gym. You were also quiet." Since the expectations for hallway behavior were the same for everyone in the school, the children received consistent feedback about what they were doing well from many different adults.

Adults become hallway greeters

As the children were learning and practicing self-control in the hallways, the adults in the school were preparing for their new role as hallway greeters. Teachers at Dame who held Morning Meeting in their classrooms had already noticed the powerful effect that greetings could have on children at the beginning of the day: how being greeted by a teacher or classmate assured each child that he or she belonged in the classroom and was welcome. By having morning greeters, the leadership team hoped to extend that experience out into the school's hallways, so that children would feel welcome from the time they walked into the school. (To learn about Morning Meeting, see *The Morning Meeting Book* by Roxann Kriete, NEFC, 2002.)

Therefore, the leadership team asked the adults in the school to be in the hallways greeting children as they entered the building in the morning. Using a friendly tone and making eye contact with the children, adult greeters welcome as many children by name as possible. They also remind children who get off track what walking through the hallway should look and sound like. Principal Ed Barnwell explains that a hallway greeter's role is "very different from hallway monitoring. Monitors watch, but don't engage, and they usually focus on punishment for misbehavior. We know you can't punish kids into learning social skills."

BENEFITS

Since Dame School began teaching hallway behavior and having greeters in the hallways, "things have been much calmer and happier," says Pat Steiner, the student support room program assistant. The number of students running through the hallways has decreased, and the noise level has dropped considerably. Adults and children start the day off feeling calmer and more connected, which leads to more productive learning days for all.

Another significant benefit of having hallway greeters is that this simple practice gives adults and children a chance to interact in an informal, positive way. Through their greetings, adults make it a point to convey excitement about the day, especially with children who may have struggled with self-control the day before. A cheerful adult greeting reminds these children that this is a new day and encourages them to keep trying. "It lets the children know that we really care about them, want to get to know them, and are ready to help them do their best," says Linda Stephenson.

Another exciting change, notes Ed Barnwell, "is that now the kids are initiating greetings and conversations. Children ask adults how their evening was, or how they're feeling that day. It's really amazing to see small children taking an interest in adults' lives. And it speaks to the kind of community we're building at Dame."

Teach expectations to children Dame School leaders might have chosen to address their arrival time challenges with a long list of "don'ts," such as "Don't run in the hallways," "Don't yell," and "Don't horse around." However, that approach wouldn't have helped students understand what they were supposed to do, and it would have started the day out on a punitive, rather than a positive, note. It also would have been a confusing contrast to the positive disciplinary approach teachers were using in their classrooms. By teaching expectations thoroughly and explaining how following them would help everyone at school, adults at Dame help the children learn to manage their own behavior, ensure consistency in teaching approaches inside and outside the classrooms, and achieve their goal of creating a welcoming atmosphere for the beginning of the day.

Provide adults with as much direction as needed When this initiative started, the leadership team provided school staff with respectful guidance and reminders about effective ways to greet the children, emphasizing the value of a consistent approach. This helped ensure that all the hallway greeters understood what was expected of them.

At one point, when the leadership team noticed that hallway greeters were "clumping up" in the hallways, they asked support staff to station themselves in certain areas and classroom teachers to stand at their doors so that the adults would be spread throughout the building at arrival time. Now that the routine has been in place for several years, there's less need for such a specific structure. Now any available adult acts as a hallway greeter, and having friendly adult greeters throughout the corridors is simply part of life at Dame.

Review and reteach regularly Routines need to be retaught at the beginning of each year. At Dame, each class reviews expectations for hallway behavior and practices the routine during the first weeks of school. Adult hallway greeters get a friendly reminder about how to do their part at the year's first all-staff meeting. This approach ensures that children know exactly what is expected of them and that they understand the connection between their behavior and the goal of calm, safe hallways.

Daily Message Board

Beginning the day by reading all-school news

PURPOSE

To welcome children, parents, and teachers to school in a way that emphasizes learning and community

G abe, a third grader, bounds through the door into the foyer of Chilmark School and heads right for the message board. He joins Sophie, a first grader, who is reading the day's message with her mother:

Good Morning!

It's the 100th day of school. We'll all celebrate this afternoon by doing special activities, games, and art projects about the number 100. What is your class doing?

Today's Morning Circle challenge: Make a K-1-2-3-4-5 pattern.

Sophie's mother asks Gabe what his class is doing for the 100th day celebration, and he shares enthusiastically and then asks Sophie what her class has planned.

"Sounds like it will be a great day!" says Sophie's mother to both children, who head off to their classrooms full of anticipation.

When students, parents, and teachers enter Chilmark School in the morning, they immediately make their way to the whiteboard in the entryway and read the message written on it. The message is typically composed of a sentence or two about the day

---

Chilmark School, Chilmark, Massachusetts
rural; public ▪ K–5 ▪ 60 students ▪ 3 multi-age classrooms ▪ one of several schools serving year-round residents of the island of Martha's Vineyard

The wording and topics for all-school messages are selected carefully so they will be engaging for students at all grade levels.

ahead and a "circle challenge," which tells students how to arrange themselves later at Chilmark's daily all-school meeting. (See "Morning Circle" on page 79.) The routine of stopping to read the message helps children settle down and focus, brings together students of different ages, gives them a meaningful reading experience, and increases parents' sense of connection to the school.

Chilmark's teachers and principal take turns writing the message each day. The format is similar to the daily morning message each teacher writes for her or his class; it begins with a friendly greeting, followed by a couple of sentences about school news. Often there is a question or some other interactive element. (To learn more about morning messages for classrooms, see *The Morning Meeting Book* by Roxann Kriete, NEFC, 2002 and *Morning Meeting Messages, K–6: 180 Sample Charts from Three Classrooms* by Fisher et al, NEFC, 2006.

The wording and topics for all-school messages are selected carefully so they will be engaging for students at all grade levels. "The all-school message usually gives information about what's happening that day," says K–1 teacher Robin Smith, "schoolwide events, what's going on in classrooms, or other news." The interactive elements are related to the news and invite school members to make connections, as in the opening scene, where the question about plans for 100th day celebration got Gabe, Sophie, and Sophie's mother talking.

Because Chilmark's sixty students come to school on foot, by bus, or with parents during a twenty-five minute window at the beginning of the day, the area around the announcement board is rarely crowded, and each student has time to read the daily message. Everyone enters through the school's front door, which leads into a large foyer where the all-school message is placed. The whiteboard occupies a prominent spot at the children's eye level and is situated so that small groups can easily gather around and read it together.

BENEFITS

Robin Smith says that since Chilmark started using an all-school message, "calmness starts the day." This routine helps children enter school with a purpose. Rather than running to their classrooms, they pause, read, converse, and connect, all of which help smooth the transition from home to school. Starting the day this way also underscores the importance of reading; children are motivated to read the message because they want to know what it says.

Reading the all-school message also helps students of different ages get to know each other. Older children help younger classmates by reading the message aloud or guiding them in sounding out words, and the content of the message sparks conversations. This routine creates a daily opportunity for children to listen to each other and practice cooperation.

The announcement board connects parents with school life by providing information and giving them an opportunity to interact with students of all ages. "Parents love knowing more about what's going on across grade levels," says Ms. Smith.

KEYS TO SUCCESS

Prevent overcrowding at the message board Chilmark's way of doing a school-wide message works well for them because students don't all arrive at the same time. Everyone has ample time to read the message before the day begins. Other ways to achieve similar results might include posting duplicate messages in multiple places, or using a public announcement system to deliver a community-building morning message. (See "Morning Announcements" on the next page.)

Keep messages focused on community building Ms. Smith emphasizes the importance of using "language that develops a sense of cooperation and community" in all-school messages. All-school messages should make everyone feel welcome and should focus on what's happening currently in the school, so they aren't a good place to recognize individual accomplishments or to remind parents about logistics.

Morning Announcements

Designed to set a positive, unifying tone

At many schools, there's no central place to display an all-school morning message where all students will see it. An alternative is to use the public announcement system to broadcast a message that sets a positive, unifying tone for the day. Principal Karen Casto used this approach at Penn Valley Elementary School in Levittown, Pennsylvania.

Every day, promptly at 9:05, she'd go on the air, beginning with a greeting, "Good morning, Penn Valley!" and then naming the people in the school who had birthdays that day. The birthday announcements not only helped people get to know each other—they also got the children's attention because students liked seeing which of the birthday people they recognized.

A few general announcements followed, each selected carefully for its pertinence to all grade levels. "As a teacher, I had endured morning announcements that went on and on, or that were meant for specific grade levels or for staff only. I knew that people would stop listening if the announcements didn't apply to them, and that wouldn't be an upbeat way to start the day," explains Dr. Casto. At Penn Valley the content of the announcements varied from day to day, but they were always brief, focused, and relevant.

Morning announcements always concluded with words of encouragement such as *Have a great day*, *Do your best*, and *Take care of each other*. "How the day begins can impact how the rest of the day goes," says Dr. Casto. "Just as teachers set the daily tone for their classrooms, as principal, I used these words to set a positive daily tone for the school, reminding students what was expected of them and what was possible if we focused on our common goals."

Penn Valley Elementary School, Levittown, Pennsylvania
suburban; public ▪ K–5 ▪ 310 students ▪ 18 classrooms ▪ 5 self-contained special education classrooms

Learning to Do Lunch

Students and staff collaborate on developing rules and procedures for lunchtime

Recently, Simone and Khaliyah have really gotten into thumb wrestling, and today, as soon as they get to their lunch table, they push their trays aside in order to get a few rounds in before eating. When Ms. Khan, the lunch supervisor, sees the girls playing, she comes over, gets their attention, and gestures at the list of lunch rules and procedures on their table.

"We have to eat first," says Khaliyah, showing that she knows what the problem is.

Ms. Khan nods and says, "You may play when you've finished." The girls reach for their trays and settle down to lunch.

At Garfield Elementary School in Springfield, Virginia, "Eat first" is one of the lunchtime procedures developed as part of a schoolwide rule making process that helped transform this school's lunchroom atmosphere from chaotic to its current vibrant hum. Students were involved at every stage of the process, an approach that increased their willingness to live by the rules and ensured that they really knew how they were expected to behave. Here's how it worked:

School leaders decided to focus on addressing lunchtime behavior problems before school opened one year. But instead of jumping right in, they deliberately started with establishing an effective, consistent classroom-based approach to discipline. For the first months of school, the focus was on helping children create classroom rules and learn to live by those rules. "Although we were eager to begin work-

Garfield Elementary School, Springfield, Virginia
suburban; public ▪ K–6 ▪ 350 students ▪ 17 classrooms ▪ 48% of students receive free or reduced-price lunch ▪ 37 home languages ▪ high rate of student transience

ing on the lunchroom problems," says principal Maureen Marshall, "we knew our efforts would be more successful in the long run if we built on a strong foundation that started in classrooms."

During those first months of school, children and teachers in each classroom shared their hopes and goals for the year and generated classroom rules that would help everyone in the class realize his or her goals. Teachers introduced procedures that would allow the class to live by their rules, modeled them, and provided the children with lots of opportunities to practice. To help the children learn to make independent decisions in situations when there is not just one correct way of behaving, they role-played scenarios and discussed ways of behaving that fit with the rules.

Throughout this time, teachers used positive comments to reinforce appropriate behavior and introduced logical consequences that would help children learn from their mistakes. Each class also established a "time-out" area in their room for people who needed to take a break in order to regain self-control. (To learn more about the positive use of time-out and other aspects of the approach to discipline that Garfield uses, see *Rules in School* by Brady et al, NEFC, 2003.)

While this groundwork was being laid in classrooms, faculty and administrators observed at lunchtime. Garfield's lunch schedule is typical of many public elementary schools: Classes eat in thirty-minute shifts on a staggered schedule that moves 350 students through the cafeteria over the course of two hours. The observers noticed the loud, chaotic atmosphere, as well as numerous instances of students treating others, including Ms. Khan, the lunch supervisor, disrespectfully.

The intensive focus on improving lunch began in December and lasted for three months. The first step was that for two full weeks, instead of just being in the building at lunchtime, Ms. Khan stayed all day. With Janet Dougherty, Garfield's guidance counselor, she visited each of the school's seventeen classes and asked the children, "What's working at lunchtime? What's not? What would you like lunch in the cafeteria to look, sound, and feel like?"

The children had lots of ideas. Many of them said they wanted lunchtime to be less rowdy. They voiced concerns about bullying, disruptive behavior, and rules that seemed to be enforced inconsistently. Ms. Khan and Ms. Dougherty listened carefully to each class's ideas and wrote them down on large sheets of chart paper.

Next, Ms. Khan and Ms. Dougherty took the information they'd gathered to the Student Cooperative Association (SCA), an elected group of about twenty fourth, fifth, and sixth graders. Using a process similar to the one students at the school use to make their classroom rules, the SCA members organized the ideas into common themes. They found that most of the ideas fit under one of three themes: Respect Yourself; Respect Others; and Respect the Environment. These became the new Garfield lunch rules.

Next, staff designed lunch-room procedures that would foster the atmosphere of respect called for by the new rules. These guidelines state specifically how students are expected to move around the cafeteria, eat, and clean up. There are also procedures for adults to follow when students break the rules. For instance, part of the new lunch-room discipline policy says that a student who is not following the rules will be reminded of them, but only once. If the student continues to misbehave, she or he will be directed to leave the table and finish eating at one of several desks placed around the edge of the room for students who need a break from their classmates.

Teachers used positive comments to reinforce appropriate behavior and introduced logical consequences that would help children learn from their mistakes.

Teachers introduced the new procedures to the members of the Student Cooperative Association, and then those children modeled them for the rest of the student body at an all-school assembly. The students also did role plays to show ideas for situations in which there are numerous possible appropriate ways to behave: for example, they showed what "eating with good manners" and "cooperating with others" could look like. The presentation was videotaped so it could be used for review in the future.

Finally, before the rules and procedures were officially implemented, each class visited the cafeteria during a scheduled guidance period to practice the procedures and to do some role playing for themselves. For instance, they practiced placing trash carefully in the bin when Ms. Khan wheeled it to their table, using inside voices, pushing in chairs, and responding to the "lights off" signal for silence. They role-played ways of behaving in specific scenarios that required independent decision making, such as deciding what to do if they finished eating sooner than others at their table. Once children had completed this hands-on experience, they were expected to follow the lunch rules and procedures.

To ensure that the rules and procedures students and staff crafted will endure, a review is now included among beginning-of-the-year activities at Garfield. The video-taped examples of students modeling expected behaviors are updated as needed and shown during an annual all-school spirit assembly on the lunch rules, and each class visits the cafeteria to practice lunch procedures.

Since making these changes, lunch has become a more enjoyable experience for everyone at Garfield. "It's not perfect, but it's much better," says Dr. Marshall, the principal, noting that she's getting fewer discipline referrals from the lunchroom.

The process has increased students' respect for Ms. Khan and made her more effective in her role. "We've always talked about how Ms. Khan has the biggest classroom in the school," says Dr. Marshall, "but having her spend time in classrooms really helped the children start perceiving her as a teacher." An added benefit was that by visiting classrooms Ms. Khan got to know the children better and was able to observe the discipline methods classroom teachers used.

The expectations for lunchtime behavior and consequences for misbehavior are fair and are applied consistently. Ms. Dougherty, the guidance counselor, says that because the whole community was involved in creating and learning the new lunch rules, adults at the school feel confident that "the children really do understand what's expected of them. The children are motivated to follow the new rules because the rules are connected to what they said they want the cafeteria to be like." When problems do come up, staff members say that simply pointing to the copy of the rules on the table is often enough to help a child who has lost self-control get back on track.

KEYS TO SUCCESS

Groundwork laid first in classrooms Dr. Marshall believes that the school's decision to wait until classroom rules and discipline were in place before beginning schoolwide work on lunch rules was crucial. It allowed the school to model the lunchroom rule making and rule-teaching process on the classroom rules process that students were already familiar with. Because teachers use a consistent approach to classroom discipline, this mirroring of lunch and classroom processes also helped all teachers approach lunchtime discipline in a consistent, effective way.

Involvement of student leaders Both Dr. Marshall and Ms. Dougherty say that engaging members of the Student Cooperative Association in the process of crafting the rules and then having them act as role models for their peers was a very successful strategy. "Having student leaders demonstrate the expected behaviors was very powerful," says Dr. Marshall. "The SCA members are popular kids, and their example carried a lot of weight with their classmates."

Collaboration for a common purpose Perhaps the most important key was that Garfield's approach to improving the lunchroom climate engaged stakeholders from throughout the school in ways that encouraged them to grow and to see each other differently. Administrators and teachers spent time in the lunchroom and became more invested in what happened there. Lunch staff learned about classroom practice and listened to children's ideas. Student leaders collaborated with adults to find ways to make lunchtime more comfortable for their classmates. The end result was a school that felt more unified.

Bus Communities

Teachers lead an effort to improve bus behavior and build community among bus riders

PURPOSE

To make time on the school bus safer and more pleasant for children and bus drivers

ifth grade teacher Martha Hanley surveys the group of thirty-five third, fourth, and fifth graders gathered in her classroom for the first bus group meeting of the year and says, "Welcome, riders of Bus Number 2! My name is Ms. Hanley, and I'll be your bus teacher this year. We'll be working together to make sure that everyone has as many good days on the bus as possible. To start, who wants to share an idea about what makes a good day on the bus for you?" Half a dozen hands shoot up.

At Grafton Elementary School, every student is assigned to a bus. "That means fifteen buses with all the usual problems, including bullying," says fifth grade teacher Martha Hanley. Recognizing that children's experiences on the bus affect their ability to learn in school, she and seven other teachers formed a study group focused on improving bus behavior, and then volunteered to be "bus teachers," adults who helped students and drivers solve problems that came up on the bus. Their efforts to build bus communities included working with students to create bus rules. At the end of the first year, after bus incidents had decreased significantly, school leaders at Grafton decided to formally adopt the program and expand it to include more staff.

Starting with student rule making

The process began when members of the study group read about how other schools had addressed bus problems in *Creating a Safe and Friendly School* (Northeast Foundation for Children, 2006). After considering which ideas could be adapted for a school of their size and grade range, they decided that having students create bus rules was a good place to start. They also decided that rather than creating a set of rules for all buses, it made the most sense at their school for each bus to create its own set of rules.

Grafton Elementary School, Grafton, Massachusetts
suburban; public ■ grades 3-5 ■ 707 students ■ 33 classrooms ■ 10% of students receive free or reduced-priced lunch
■ 10-12 classrooms at each grade level

Bus 1 Rules

Our behavior is appropriate for the bus:

1. We are nice to each other.

2. We are respectful, polite, and welcoming.

3. We are safe on Bus 1. We keep our hands to ourselves.

Bus 2 Rules

1. Be safe. Sit and keep hands to yourself.

2. Be friendly, respectful, and cooperative.

3. Help each other follow the rules.

Rules created by two of Grafton Elementary School's bus groups

Each member of the study group assigned herself to be the bus teacher for one or two buses. Then each bus teacher arranged for her bus riders to come to a twenty-minute meeting with her early in the school year—one meeting per bus group. At these meetings, the children got to know each other better, shared ideas about what good days on the bus were like, and produced a short, general list of rules that, if followed, would result in more good days on the bus. (See "Creating Schoolwide Rules," p. 34, and "Learning to Do Lunch," p. 53, to read more about rule making with mixed-age groups.)

The rule making approach they used was adapted from the process Grafton teachers use with students to create classroom rules. In both settings, involving students in rule creation helps them feel more invested in the rules. Also in both settings, the rules are a few statements that emphasize what children should do, such as "Be respectful to yourself and others" and "Be safe," rather than a long list of No's, as in "No hitting" or "No standing in the aisle." As with classroom rules, no two bus groups' rules were exactly the same. "Having rules for their bus in their own words makes them more meaningful," says Ms. Hanley, "and even though each bus ended up with slightly different rules, they all covered similar ideas about being safe, respectful, and kind to others." The students were told that each bus driver would be given a copy of that bus's rules to keep on the bus.

Because the children were still expected to follow the "Bus Riders' Code of Conduct" in the Garfield student/parent handbook, the bus teachers helped children to understand that the code's requirements, such as "Sit down when the bus is moving," fit with the children's own rules about being safe and respectful.

The bus teachers concluded by explaining that they would continue to be their group's bus teacher for the rest of the year, which meant that they'd check in with them from time to time about how things were going on the bus. If any problems came up, the students were told, they were to let their bus teacher know by putting a note in that teacher's mailbox or finding that teacher during the school's daily ten minute morning break.

Involving the bus drivers

Next, the study group members followed up with the bus drivers, explaining their new bus teacher role and presenting each driver with his or her bus's student-created rules. In addition, they introduced a new system for drivers to report problems on the bus.

Before, bus drivers had reported all problems to the office; in the new system they would report their problem to their bus teacher instead, and she would handle the problem with that group of students and bring it to the attention of administrators as appropriate. Ms. Hanley noticed that some bus drivers started communicating a lot more as a result. "Some drivers were reluctant to report minor problems to the office, because they didn't want to get the kids into trouble. Telling the bus teacher was not as big a deal, so we heard about more issues as they came up. That made it possible for us to address problems before they escalated."

Bus teachers followed up on reports of trouble in ways that emphasized problem solving. They met with students individually, in small groups, or as an entire bus group and guided the students in applying the same conflict resolution techniques and problem solving meeting formats they were learning to use in school.

Bus teachers also checked in informally with bus riders and drivers just to see how things were going, and at midyear, they gathered each bus group and took another look at the bus rules they'd made. After assessing how well the rules were working, some groups made adjustments; for all groups, the midyear meeting helped keep the rules meaningful and fresh.

Learning from the pilot period

As the year continued, the study group devoted some time to reflecting on the successes and challenges of their pilot effort. Everyone agreed that the bus communities program should continue, but they also acknowledged that it had taken a lot of their time. They saw that if the program were to continue, it would need to be restructured to make the workload more manageable.

They recommended therefore that in the second year of the program, almost all of the teachers in the school become bus teachers. This meant that each bus group would have three bus teachers, who would share responsibilities. Each bus group would meet with their bus teachers early in the year to create their bus rules, then gather twice each marking period to continue community-building activities and problem solving on bus issues. To minimize planning time for the teachers, the original study group would create an outline for each meeting. Finally, a group of four adults—Ms. Hanley, assistant principal Leigh Petrowsky, and two other teachers—would be the designated "go to" people if any teacher needed help with solving a bus problem.

The administrators, impressed by how much bus problems had declined during the program's pilot period, supported these recommendations. The school's teachers were willing to try the program because they could share bus teacher responsibilities and get help with any serious problems, they'd receive meeting outlines to simplify their planning, and time for bus meetings would be built into the school schedule. Most of all, they had seen the value of the bus program during the pilot year. Students were arriving at school calmer and more ready to learn, and when problems did come up, there was a system for addressing them that didn't take away from instructional time.

"With this approach, we are headed in the right direction," says Ms. Hanley. "Now we'll be able to have all the bus groups meet regularly, to start earlier in the year, and to involve many more teachers without taking a lot of their time."

BENEFITS

This bus initiative has had a positive impact on bus behavior. Office referrals have dropped, and problems are resolved more quickly. Bus incidents inevitably distract children from their classroom work, so improvements in this area have had a positive impact on learning as well. Martha Hanley explains, "Children can concentrate better when they know that a problem will be worked on in a caring way, without blame and shame. After talking with students about bus problems, I could see their agitation ease. Even though we didn't solve all of the problems all of the time, the students knew that they had help, and that made for a better learning environment."

In their role as liaisons between bus drivers and the school, and between students and bus drivers, bus teachers help everyone in the community stay focused on the common goal of "more good days on the bus for everyone." Their work sends a clear message that this community is committed to making the school a safe and caring place, and that time spent on the bus is part of being at school.

Because children from a mix of grades ride each bus, the bus communities program provides opportunities for children of different ages to work together, and for teachers to interact with students outside of their classes. In a large school like Grafton, with at least ten classrooms at each grade level, this program offers a welcome opportunity for cross-age learning.

KEYS TO SUCCESS

Piloted by a small, committed group The members of the study group that piloted this effort at Grafton were motivated because they chose this project for themselves. "Starting out with a group of people who really wanted to do it" was important, says Ms. Hanley. "As a small group we were willing and able to work through the kinks that are a part of starting anything new."

Built on familiar routines and established foundations The study group designed an approach that capitalized on routines and skills that were already in place at Grafton. For instance, students were already familiar with the meeting formats they used and had experience participating in discussions from their classrooms. They used a rule making process and steps to conflict resolution that were already being used successfully in other areas of the school. This consistency simplified planning for teachers and showed students that skills learned in the classroom are applicable in other settings as well.

Supported by administrators and colleagues Support from the school community was vital to this project's success. From the beginning, the administrators approved the study group's use of professional development time to research and plan this project. During the pilot period, colleagues provided coverage during the study group's meetings with bus riders.

Work shared among many When the program rolled out to involve the whole faculty, it was vital that supports were built in to keep each individual teacher's responsibilities manageable. Although everyone valued efforts to decrease bus problems, the program may not have survived had there not been deliberate changes to keep workloads feasible.

"As a small group we were willing and able to work through the kinks that are a part of starting anything new."

Growth guided by goals At the end of the pilot period, the study group was, rightfully, excited by the success of their initial efforts. As they reflected on their first year of work, they made an honest assessment of the program's strengths and weaknesses and adjusted their plans for going forward accordingly. In addition to restructuring the program to share responsibility among more teachers, they set longer range goals for the future, such as involving bus drivers more actively and helping students get to know their bus drivers better.

Dismissal Time

A calm, orderly send-off with a personal touch

PURPOSE

To make dismissal time a smooth, positive experience for the whole school

It's the end of the day in Ms. Overstreet's fourth grade class. When everyone has packed up, Ms. Overstreet leads the class down the hallway toward the front door. Seeing that Ms. Conz's first grade class is already there, she stops the fourth graders a few paces back to prevent crowding. The students wait, chatting quietly, adjusting backpacks and zipping up coats.

After a few moments it's their turn to exit. Ms. Overstreet stands by the open front door and gives each child a quick, friendly "high five" as he or she passes through. The children climb onto buses, into cars, and head off on foot. Ms. Overstreet smiles as she heads back to her classroom.

Four Corners staff developed this simple routine for dismissal more than ten years ago to move all 229 students out the front door in an efficient and orderly fashion, and to end the school day on a positive note for teachers and students.

To reduce the bottleneck that formed at the main door, they decided that teachers would walk their classes out, and that one class would exit at a time. Instead of dismissing all students simultaneously, teachers would bring their classes out as they were ready between 2:50 and 3:00.

Another challenge was that multiple classes often converged at the spot where the school's two main hallways merged. The solution was that teachers would stop their lines and classes would take turns exiting, with one class from each side going out at a time. The teachers' way of negotiating this turn-taking with each other would provide students with a model of courtesy and respect.

Four Corners Elementary School, Greenfield, Massachusetts
small city in a rural area; public ▪ K–4 ▪ 229 students ▪ 12 classrooms ▪ 54% of students receive reduced-price or free lunch

Having teachers say a quick, personal goodbye to each student was a natural extension of the way Four Corners already used greetings at arrival time and in classroom Morning Meetings. School staff had already seen the powerful positive effect a warm greeting from an adult could have on a child's day, so it made sense to them that sending children off with a friendly goodbye could be equally beneficial. They chose a gentle "high five" because it was quick, playful, and interactive, creating a moment of connection between the teacher and each student.

Four Corners' dismissal routine makes this potentially chaotic time of day orderly and efficient.

As they would when teaching any new routine, Four Corners teachers "taught dismissal" by showing students what each part of the journey was supposed to look, sound, and feel like. Then students practiced the new routine, while the adults watched and named specifically what children were doing well, such as "I noticed that your hands stayed at your sides when you walked down the hallway today." Because the expectations for moving through the hallways were the same schoolwide, any adult could offer such reinforcement or provide reminders when students needed them.

The dismissal routine caught on quickly. In the years since the routine began, "teaching dismissal" has become a part of Four Corners' schoolwide curriculum for the first weeks of school.

BENEFITS

Four Corners' dismissal routine makes this potentially chaotic time of day orderly and efficient. On a typical day, it takes about ten minutes for twelve classes to exit the building. Because all students pack up and leave together by class, dismissal time is less rushed and children are less likely to miss their buses. Teachers check off their names on a list after they've high fived all of their students, so principal Gail Healy knows when all the classes have been dismissed, and she can wave the buses to go.

Walking down the hallway together and doing high fives at the door creates a relaxed atmosphere and ends the day on a positive note for students and teachers. Time spent waiting while another class exits allows teachers to touch base with students informally, and for students to chat and wave to friends in other classes. Many staff members help out at dismissal time as well, making this a daily time when the whole school community comes together.

Over the years, Four Corners' dismissal routine has become part of school culture. Ms. Healy points out that the routine is now so well integrated that when they teach dismissal procedures, teachers know they can ask returning students to model expectations for children who are new to the school.

KEYS TO SUCCESS

The whole staff is involved Collaborative visioning and problem solving led this school to a coordinated approach. Ms. Healy says that getting all staff involved from the beginning was a key to success. They started with discussions at staff meetings about how they wanted dismissal time to be, and they agreed that improving traffic flow was their main goal. They arrived at the new dismissal procedures after identifying trouble spots and brainstorming for solutions as a group. "Decide what you will do as a whole staff," says Ms. Healy. "It's important that everyone feels ownership and agrees to give it a try."

Foundational skills were in place first Four Corners was able to implement their dismissal routine fairly quickly because the children already had most of the requisite skills, and the school already had schoolwide standards for hallway behavior and greetings. For example, all the children knew how to walk safely in line, how to wait respectfully, and how to do a gentle high five because their classes had focused on learning these and other skills during the first weeks of the school year and had been practicing them ever since. Also, the adults at school were already all using a common approach to teaching new routines that involved interactive modeling and practice. All this foundational work made it easier to introduce a new practice and have it take hold. (To learn more about interactive modeling, see *Rules in School*, Brady et al, NEFC, 2003.)

Scale and size match the school At Four Corners, all children are dismissed out a single front door, and the whole process takes a manageable ten minutes. Other schools may need different ways to organize dismissal to meet the same goals of efficiency, orderliness, and friendliness. For example, a school that uses separate exits for bus riders and walkers might have adults other than teachers take part of the class to one door while the classroom teacher takes the rest of the class to another door.

Discussion and Planning Questions

These questions are intended for use by groups such as school leadership teams, parent-teacher partnerships, and cross-grade committees who have chosen to work together on building schoolwide community.

The suggestions on these pages are intended to help guide your group through the process of considering, planning, and implementing routines at your school.

Before choosing a routine to focus on:

Assess Look for places and times at your school where having a routine might help things go better.

- What do you notice?

- What, specifically, are the problems?

- How might a routine help?

Envision Imagine what each place and time could be like, ideally. Then choose one to focus on and develop a routine that will help achieve this vision.

- What is the vision? What are your goals?

- What will students be doing?

- What will adults be doing?

- What else needs to happen to make the vision a reality?

Take stock Decide which skills, knowledge, and procedures need to be in place before you start using your new routine. Make a plan for building those skills and practicing procedures in classroom or smaller groups.

- What do students and staff already know how to do?

- What needs to be taught? To whom? By whom?

Once you have selected a routine:

Introduce Make sure all who will be involved understand the reason for having a routine and their role in it.

- How will you introduce the routine to staff?

- How will you introduce it to students?

- Does this change need to be shared with students' families? If so, how will you do so?

Teach the routine Model the behavior you want to see. Ask learners to observe closely and describe what they notice in detail.

- How will you model the routine?

- What do you want the observers to notice?

Practice and reinforce Provide learners with opportunities to practice the routine before holding them to it. Watch them carefully and point out what they are doing well.

- How will the routine be practiced?

- How will participants get feedback?

Afterwards:

Monitor Plan to observe and check in with participants frequently.

- How will you gather information about how the routine is working?

Evaluate Take time to reflect on whether the routine you've established accomplishes the goals you set.

- What positive changes have adults and students noticed?

- How will you share that good news?

- What adjustments are needed?

Review Plan to reteach the routine on a regular basis, at least once a year.

- How and when will expectations for this routine be reviewed?

Gatherings

Gatherings, those times when the school or a part of the school comes together to work toward a common goal, celebrate academic and other accomplishments, or simply have fun, are powerful drivers of community building. Whether it's an all-school meeting or a cross-age reading time, gathering as a community helps students and staff see themselves as part of something larger than their classrooms. These are times when the values of a community are visibly displayed, inviting individuals to look around and notice, "This is who we are, this is what we believe in, this is what I'm a part of."

Gatherings that foster such a sense of belonging are built on a foundation of common knowledge and on everyday school routines. When gatherings include a mix of grade levels and offer students opportunities to play active, leading roles, they have the potential to strengthen the community even more. They help community members of all ages to know each other better and to deepen their relationships through shared experience.

Of course, simply gathering a large group doesn't build community in and of itself. Gatherings that build community are usually carefully planned and organized to ensure that they are purposeful, engaging, and appropriate for all. Because they run smoothly, students, staff, and administrators are more likely to see the event as valuable and worth the time. School leaders can offer crucial support for such gatherings by scheduling time for them, providing planning time for staff, and helping with logistics. They also need to be willing and able to clearly articulate the benefits of school gatherings to the school's extended community, including families and district leadership.

In this section you'll read about gatherings that take place during the regular school day at a variety of schools, including different types of all-school meetings, a grade level meeting, and a cross-age buddy program. All of these gatherings share some common characteristics:

■ They occur regularly—daily, weekly, or monthly.

■ Students are active participants, often assuming leadership roles.

■ Gatherings build on schoolwide common knowledge and established routines.

■ Gatherings include clear connections to academic learning and goals.

■ Gatherings are focused, purposeful, and fun. They build a sense of connection among children and adults.

As you read, think about what gatherings could be like at your school. Use the ideas here as springboards, and then turn to the discussion and planning questions at the end of the section to continue thinking through how this element of community building might be applied at your school.

SECTION THREE

Gatherings

All-School Meeting

Monthly schoolwide gatherings use
a familiar format from the classroom

Each month, everyone at K.T. Murphy gathers for an all-school meeting. This month's meeting, led by the first graders, starts with a pre-arranged greeting in which each grade represents a different insect. At the first graders' cue, all the fourth graders say, "Good morning, fifth graders," as they make big biting motions in the air to represent mosquitoes. The fifth graders reply and then greet the kindergartners, hopping in place to represent grasshoppers. The greeting travels from grade to grade around the room, accompanied by gestures of stinging and flying, as well as by smiles and laughter.

In a school with over 500 students and more than eighty staff, it can be difficult to get to know one another. At K.T. Murphy Elementary School in Stamford, Connecticut, one way staff and administrators address this is by holding monthly all-school meetings. The format is adapted from Morning Meeting, a routine that each class in the school uses to begin every day. (To learn more about daily classroom Morning Meetings, see *The Morning Meeting Book* by Roxann Kriete, NEFC, 2002.)

Like Morning Meetings in the classroom, K.T. Murphy's all-school meetings have four distinct parts: greeting, sharing, activity, and morning message. The routine is designed to help the children feel welcome; to provide them with opportunities to practice listening, empathy, and cooperation; and to include curricular connections that amplify learning.

For instance, the all-school meeting described above continued with each grade sharing about recent learnings in science, beginning with a group of first graders who shared about their study of insects. Next, representatives from a different first grade

---

K.T. Murphy Elementary School, Stamford, Connecticut
urban; public ▪ K–5 ▪ 530 students ▪ 27 classrooms ▪ 49% of students receive free or reduced-price lunch ▪ English is a second language for 38% of students

> "For some children, having more people become familiar faces really makes school feel like a safer place."

class led the activity, a variation on "head, shoulders, knees, and toes," using the vocabulary words "head," "thorax," and "abdomen." Finally, first graders led the reading of the morning message, shown using an overhead projector so everyone could read along.

Before each all-school meeting at K.T. Murphy ends, there's a drawing to determine which grade will lead the next one. This is always a highly anticipated moment in the meeting. With children beating out a drum roll on the floor, an envelope is drawn. When the winner is announced, the room erupts into clapping, squeals, and whoops.

BENEFITS

Just as classroom Morning Meetings build community among class members, these all-school meetings build a sense of schoolwide community. "For some children, having more people become familiar faces really makes school feel like a safer place," says third grade teacher Toni D'Agostino. Principal Kathy Pfister adds, "It helps us to know who we are and where we're headed together."

Planning and leading the meeting builds confidence and leadership skills for students. Every class plays a part in hosting at least one all-school meeting each year, and although teachers guide every step of the planning and practice, students actually run the meeting, using a microphone to speak in front of more than 500 people and moving them from one segment to the next by using the schoolwide signal to call for quiet attention.

KEYS TO SUCCESS

Uses a familiar format Since classroom Morning Meetings are an everyday routine at K.T. Murphy, using that familiar format to structure all-school meetings simplifies planning. Students and teachers already know how each part of Morning Meeting goes, so adapting this familiar routine for a large group is much easier than creating a format from scratch. Furthermore, since each grade level includes several classes, each class takes responsibility for just the part of the meeting their grade leads.

Ample time to prepare Still, careful preparation is required for these meetings to be successful. At K.T. Murphy, grade level teachers are sometimes provided substitute coverage so they can make initial plans. The teachers then meet with the students to finalize details, and they send out an agenda to the rest of the faculty before the meeting. If necessary, student representatives visit classrooms throughout the school to teach the greeting and the activity they're planning to do. Finally, all classroom teachers review expectations for behavior at all-school meetings with their students before they leave for the gymnasium on the day of the meeting.

Clear connections to academics Time spent planning for and participating in all-school meetings is learning time. All-school meetings provide incredible opportunities for students to reflect on and present their learning to their peers. For instance, in the all-school meeting described in the opening scene, the first grade team integrated the planning of the meeting with the culmination of a science unit exploring insects, providing a powerful opportunity for first graders to share what they'd learned with the whole school.

Grade Level Meetings

A monthly gathering of ten classes

At a large school, bringing all students together for meetings can be impractical. Faced with this situation, the fifth grade team at Grafton Elementary School in Grafton, Massachusetts holds monthly meetings for all ten of the school's fifth grade classes instead. These grade level meetings have many of the same benefits as all-school meetings, but for a more manageably-sized group of about 250 students. "We have fun, share our learning, and celebrate our progress and accomplishments," says teacher Martha Hanley.

Classes gather in the gym, where students sit in concentric circles radiating out from a podium. The meeting format is patterned after classroom Morning Meetings, with one class responsible for each segment. For example, at a recent meeting Ms. Hanley's class was in charge of leading the greeting. They led the group through a "category greeting" using categories the students had chosen, such as "If your birth date is a prime number, stand up and greet three people who are also standing."

A different class leads the sharing segment, in which several students from that class present something they've worked on recently in school. Then another class leads a quick cooperative activity, followed by birthday songs for the people celebrating birthdays that month. The meeting ends with announcements that are meaningful to the whole fifth grade.

With careful planning, these grade level meetings are completed in twenty-five minutes, the same amount of time Grafton teachers devote to classroom Morning Meetings. "We try to keep things simple so the meeting doesn't feel rushed. Teachers and students leave these monthly gatherings feeling proud and excited about our community," says Ms. Hanley.

Grafton Elementary School, Grafton, Massachusetts
suburban; public ■ grades 3–5 ■ 707 students ■ 33 classrooms ■ 10–12 classrooms at each grade level

Morning Moments

A quick, unifying all-school gathering
marks the end of each week

PURPOSE

To provide the
school with a
time to gather
as a community
in a quick but
meaningful way

By 8:30, there are more than 250 children in the large, bright room that serves as a combined cafeteria/meeting space for the International Charter School. Most have settled into eighteen class groups on the floor, and when curriculum coordinator Kerry Tuttlebee blows into a harmonica, the room quiets and all eyes turn to her. Ms. Tuttlebee says, "Good morning! Today Ruben, Elisabeth, and João will lead the singing." The day's three song leaders step forward to begin the meeting.

A scene like this one takes place each Friday at the International Charter School (ICS), when students and staff gather for a brief before-school meeting. Singing together in three languages—English, Spanish, and Portuguese—is always part of the routine. Meetings typically take about ten minutes and may also include announcements, quick activities, or greetings. Afterwards, students participate in a more in-depth Morning Meeting in classrooms. At the weekly all-school gathering, says Ms. Tuttlebee, "the point is really to just take a few moments out of our busy school life to connect with each other in a fun way."

These gatherings often include a segment when a class shares about what they have been learning. For example, fifth graders might present graphs they'd made to represent voting results, or first, second, and third graders might demonstrate dances they'd learned while studying Brazilian Carnivale.

Such presentations are scheduled beforehand. Over the years that Ms. Tuttlebee has been coordinating all-school meetings at ICS, the system has evolved. At first, classes were assigned dates to share, but once the routine was established, teachers started volunteering. Now Ms. Tuttlebee fills out the schedule by keeping track of what's going on in classrooms and making suggestions to teachers about things they might share. She makes sure that each class shares at some point during the year.

International Charter School, Pawtucket, Rhode Island
urban; public charter ▪ K–5 ▪ 270 students ▪ 18 classrooms ▪ 80% of students receive reduced-price or free lunch
▪ students are enrolled in one of two bilingual programs: Spanish/English or Portuguese/English

At International Charter School, the Friday all-school gatherings provide a welcome breather, punctuating the end of each week with an opportunity for students and staff alike to pause and connect. Deliberately brief and designed to be fun, they are a tradition everyone looks forward to.

Furthermore, Ms. Tuttlebee explains that because the school has two bilingual strands, Spanish/English and Portuguese/English, this weekly time together is vital for reinforcing a unified identity for the school. "In their daily routines and classrooms, the children's experience is almost exclusively bilingual (Spanish/English or Portuguese/English). But learning songs in English, Spanish, and Portuguese and singing them together on Fridays underscores that all three languages are equally important in our community."

These weekly meetings also provide teachers and students with opportunities to share their work with the whole school. Over the years that they've been doing this, "it's definitely become more natural for people to get up and speak in front of a large group," says Ms. Tuttlebee.

KEYS TO SUCCESS

A balance of familiar and new ICS uses a fairly consistent structure for its all-school meetings, but varies the elements enough to keep things fun. For instance, beginning the meeting by singing together is a practiced and familiar routine. However, to keep this element fresh, they change songs every few months. Classes learn new songs in English, Spanish, and Portuguese during Morning Meetings before they sing them together as a school.

A pace that fits Although coordinating weekly meetings requires a good deal of behind-the-scenes work, Ms. Tuttlebee says it's manageable because she keeps the meetings simple and brief. "Having one great meeting a week is the right pace for us right now. It makes gathering everyone together less of a production than it would be if we did it once a month. Since our purpose is to enjoy being together, this is a case where doing less more often works best."

Morning Circle

A daily gathering led by children

PURPOSE

To bring the whole school together and start each day on a positive, unified note

W hen the morning bell rings, children stream into the spacious entryway of Chilmark School. Within minutes, sixty students, their teachers, and a few visitors have formed a large circle. Nathan, a third grader, holds a chart naming the members of his class who will be leading today's meeting. He steps forward, the circle quiets, and the meeting begins.

Every day at Chilmark School begins with Morning Circle, an all-school meeting that's led by students. Morning Circle begins with the Pledge of Allegiance, followed by the reading of that day's "Thought for the Day"—a quote that relates to current happenings in school or the world, including curriculum topics, seasonal events, and holidays. Younger students generally choose from quotes a teacher has collected for this purpose, while fourth and fifth graders use collections they have assembled.

The student who reads the quote invites others to share their ideas about what it means. Afterwards, people celebrating birthdays are named and visitors are introduced.

Next, a student leader asks if anyone has news or announcements. Any child or adult can share information they think is "newsworthy," a standard that children learn and practice in classrooms before they begin sharing news at Morning Circle. News-worthy announcements at Chilmark might include a fourth grader giving an update about the previous night's Red Sox game, the principal acknowledging a class's work on a community service project, or a teacher mentioning that her class has a field trip planned for the next day.

Occasionally, children share news that isn't newsworthy. For instance, Robin Smith, a K–1 teacher at Chilmark, recalls that right after Easter, "many children wanted to share Easter bunny stories. After a couple, we said that was enough on that

---

Chilmark School, Chilmark, Massachusetts
rural; public ■ K–5 ■ 60 students ■ 3 multi-age classrooms ■ school serves year-round residents of the island of Martha's Vineyard

> "... this is a powerful time when children of all ages learn to speak in front of a crowd and feel part of a larger community."

topic for now. In that kind of situation, we make it a point to remind the children of other places and times during the school day when they can share." In general, though, she says "this is a powerful time when children of all ages learn to speak in front of a crowd and feel part of a larger community."

Chilmark's Morning Circle ends with the whole school singing a song of the student leaders' choice. They make their selection from a collection of Morning Circle songs every community member knows, and display a pre-written chart with the words on it so visitors can follow along.

The finishing touch is that students are dismissed by categories—"If you have an older brother, walk to your classroom," "If you ate cereal for breakfast, you may go now." This fun way of staggering the flow of children back to classrooms works at Chilmark because students are accustomed to traveling through the hallways by themselves.

Preparing to lead Morning Circle

Each of the school's three multi-age classes leads Morning Circle for a week at a time. At the beginning of the year, teachers lead the meetings while students practice doing Morning Circle jobs in their classrooms. When a class is ready to lead, the laminated chart that names and describes each of the jobs is moved to their classroom. At the beginning of each day children sign up, taking turns so that several students can try each job during the week. The chart naming that day's leaders is carried to the gathering place and displayed in the circle.

BENEFITS

This daily gathering brings everyone at Chilmark together each morning to begin the day in a fun way. In these fifteen minutes, children and adults get to know each other, important news is communicated, and the sense of community at the school is reaffirmed.

Leading the meeting helps students become comfortable and confident speaking in public. Robin Smith says the experience is a powerful way for children to

Morning Circle

FLAG SALUTE
*Please place your right hand over your heart
for the Pledge of Allegiance.*

THOUGHT FOR THE DAY
*Now is the time for a moment of silence.
_____ , what is the thought for today?*

BIRTHDAYS
Is it anyone's birthday today?

NEWS AND ANNOUNCEMENTS
Who has news or announcements?

MORNING SONG
This morning's song is _____ .

DISMISSAL
*When you are dismissed, take two steps into the
circle and then return to your classroom.*

Script used by students leading Chilmark School's Morning Circle

learn responsibility. Because this is a daily routine with rotating leadership, children have many opportunities to be leaders over the course of a year.

Parents and other visitors to the school are welcome at Morning Circle. Participating helps them stay connected with what's happening at the school and gives them an informal opportunity to observe the children. "Parents are thrilled to come in and see their children running a meeting," says Ms. Smith.

Uses a simple format Making Morning Circle a predictable routine minimizes planning and helps ensure that children of all ages can lead it successfully. Although the format seldom varies, the quick pace of Chilmark's Morning Circle and the choices the student leaders make each day keep the meetings fresh and interesting. Daily meetings work best if they are simple and quick; with sixty students, Chilmark is a manageable size for such frequent gatherings.

Students are prepared through modeling and practice At the beginning of the school year, Chilmark teachers lead Morning Circle for the first few weeks, modeling the routine and each of the jobs involved in leading it. All students benefit from this review, which establishes clear expectations in a proactive manner. Students also learn the Morning Circle jobs and practice sharing "newsworthy" news in their classrooms before doing these things with the whole school.

Includes a procedure for assembling How the circle takes shape sets the tone for everything that follows. Chilmark does not leave this up to chance. At the beginning of the school year, classes practice "circling up" quickly and efficiently in the building and on the playground. Children learn to adjust their bodies so there will be room for everyone in the circle, and they are taught that "it doesn't matter who they are next to."

For Morning Circle, there is additional guidance, as students arrange themselves according to the daily "circle challenge" on the all-school message board. Typically, students are directed to make a pattern, such as "boy-girl" or "alphabetical by first name." This mixes up the grade levels and ensures that students stand next to different people at Morning Circle each day. (To learn more about Chilmark's all-school message, see "Daily Message Board" on page 49.)

PURPOSE

To provide older and younger children with opportunities to build relationships and literacy skills

Reading Buddies

Partners from three grade levels
read together each week

"What are we going to read today, Sofia?" asks Ruby, gesturing at the picture book her first grade partner is holding. The younger girl shows her fifth grade reading buddy the cover and says proudly, "I know all the words in this one."

"Let's get started then!" says Ruby, and the two nestle into a spot on the rug among several other pairs of fifth and first graders.

Each child in Puentes, the dual-language immersion program at the Regional Multicultural Magnet School (RMMS), has reading buddies from two different grade levels. Typically, teachers try to schedule about thirty minutes of buddy reading for their classes each week. Spending this time together helps students build literacy skills and strengthens cross-grade connections among children and teachers.

The dual-language immersion program at RMMS includes about 100 children in six classes, with teachers who "loop," staying with the same class for two years. For Reading Buddies, the program is split into two groups: the kindergarten, second and fourth grade classes are grouped together, as are the first, third and fifth grade classes. Each child has two reading buddies, one from each of the other grades in their group.

Teachers work together to schedule meeting times and make buddy assignments. When matching students, they consider reading skills, temperament, and native language, and they try to partner children whose abilities complement each other. In general, older readers are paired with younger students who read at a lower level, and students with weak literacy or social skills are usually not put together.

Regional Multicultural Magnet School, New London, Connecticut
urban; public magnet ▪ K–5 ▪ 500 students ▪ 28 classrooms ▪ 38% of students receive free or reduced-price lunch ▪ school includes students from twelve rural, suburban, and urban districts ▪ about 100 students are enrolled in the dual-language immersion program

> "Struggling readers in upper grades often feel very good about their reading when working with a younger child."

Buddy assignments are changed frequently, every four to six weeks, although partners who work especially well together may stay together for a longer time.

Before students read with their buddies for the first time, each teacher prepares her class. For instance, the kindergarten teacher gathers her students, and they talk about what reading with an older friend will be like. The upper grade teachers demonstrate techniques for working on reading skills with a younger partner, such as taking turns reading, searching text for letters or words, and asking comprehension questions. They also discuss ways older partners can help make buddy reading go well, such as choosing a good place to sit and how to hold a book so others can see. This coaching helps things go smoothly from the start.

Reading buddies usually gather in one classroom. Younger students bring picture books selected by their teachers, or buddies choose from the Reading Buddies section of the classroom library. Once the children settle down with their partners, their teachers check with them as needed about skills, book choice, and behavior issues. They also observe, compare notes with each other, and work out future buddy assignments.

BENEFITS

Susan Hafler, a fourth and fifth grade teacher, has noticed that both older and younger readers benefit from working with a buddy. She has noticed that "struggling readers in upper grades often feel very good about their reading when working with a younger child, and children who struggle with behavior are sometimes remarkably transformed by the opportunity to be nurturing and helpful." Her students also report that they learn from the challenge of explaining an idea or helping a child sound out a word.

Reading Buddies also helps students build relationships across grades that extend beyond the classroom. Friendships that begin with Reading Buddies continue to develop in the cafeteria and on the playground. Furthermore, by observing the kind of reading their older friend does or the kind of thinking she demonstrates, younger students learn what they can look forward to doing as they grow older.

Reading Buddies benefits teachers as well, by helping them get to know children they'll eventually have as students and allowing them to sustain relationships with students they've taught in the past. The program also gives the teachers regular opportunities to share knowledge about current and past students with each other, which makes them a stronger team.

KEYS TO SUCCESS

Teachers do their own planning Although some schools with cross-grade buddy programs build time for buddy class activities into the school schedule, at RMMS it's up to the teachers to find the time. Although they say that scheduling is a challenge, the teachers in the dual-language immersion program have kept this program going for more than ten years. They credit this to several factors, noting especially that they are a small group that works well together, they have a fair amount of control over how they use instructional time in their classrooms, and their classes have reasonably parallel schedules.

Space is adequate for the activity When two classes gather in a single room, space is at a premium. Partners need enough space to do their work, and teachers need to be able to see them. The RMMS teachers sometimes distribute students among several classrooms, but they believe that in general keeping everyone together is worth a bit of a squeeze. Children reading together don't each need their own desk or chair, but for buddy activities that require more room, gathering in the library, cafeteria, or even outside may be preferred.

Students are prepared Buddy activities work best when everyone involved understands what is expected and can meet those expectations. Reading is a common choice for buddy programs, and it often works well because partner reading is a familiar activity for most children. However, the RMMS teachers go a crucial step further by preparing students specifically for what it will be like to read with an older or younger child. By doing this before the first meeting and then checking in periodically, they help ensure that children have positive experiences with their buddies.

Discussion and Planning Questions

These questions are intended for use by groups such as school leadership teams, parent-teacher partnerships, and cross-grade committees who have chosen to work together on building schoolwide community.

The suggestions on these pages are intended to help guide your group through the process of considering, planning, and holding gatherings on a regular basis at your school.

Before choosing a specific format:

Envision Imagine what a successful gathering at your school might be like.

- Where would it take place?

- Who would be there?

- What would students be doing?

- What would adults be doing?

Be purposeful Make sure you can explain what the school community hopes to gain from working on and holding gatherings.

- What results do you hope to see?

- Who will benefit? How?

Take stock Decide which skills and procedures need to be in place for the gatherings to run smoothly. Make a plan for building skills and practicing procedures in classroom or smaller groups.

- What do students and staff know already?

- What needs to be taught? To whom? By whom?

Once you have decided on a format:

Consider logistics Think through practical details ahead of time.

- Where and when will the gathering be held?

- How does the space need to be prepared?

- Will you need any audio/visual equipment?

- How long will it take?

- How often will it be held?

- How will students be seated?

- Where will teachers, other staff, and visitors sit?

- How will arrival and dismissal be organized?

- What will the agenda be and how will people know what it is?

- How will transitions be handled during the meeting?

- What other details do you need to consider ahead of time?

Introduce the project Make sure all who will be involved understand what will be happening and their role in it.

- How will the gathering be introduced to adults?

- How will it be introduced to students?

- How will students' families be informed or included?

Start small Try to build up to holding a full-scale gathering gradually.

- What subsets could meet before the whole group gathers?

- What else could you do to help ensure success?

Prepare the students Work on building the new skills that students need specifically for the gathering.

- What do people need to know about being good audience members?

- What do they need to know about playing a role in leading a meeting?

Afterwards:

Evaluate and celebrate Take time to stop and reflect on how things are going. Think about and celebrate successes, rather than focusing only on things that need to be improved.

- Is it working the way you expected?

- Have there been any surprises?

- What has been successful?

- What could make this go better?

Update Review your purpose and goals for having gatherings.

- Has your purpose changed?

- Is it time to set different goals?

Yearly Events

Events such as field days, science fairs, festivals, or field trips can be highlights of the elementary school experience for students, and, because these special times may take place outside of the school building, they can also be occasions when the school community is especially visible to the public. Typically, students, staff, families, and community members are involved. Special events give students and teachers a chance to diverge from their ordinary routine as they work, learn, and play together for an extended time in larger, mixed-age groups.

Successful all-school events build on practices that have already been established at a school. The common knowledge that students and teachers have developed and the everyday routines they've practiced apply also to events. And regular in-school gatherings give children experience with being part of a large, mixed-age group. When high profile events go well, they powerfully demonstrate the value of the community-building work that a school has done.

In addition, when they are safe, fun, and positive for all students and staff, special events can actively strengthen school community. Achieving this requires careful planning, as well as a clear sense of purpose. When well-done, such events become part of the school's culture, traditions that everyone looks forward to each year.

In this section, you'll read about yearly events at rural, suburban, and urban schools. Each of the featured events reflects the values of its school and the particular character of its local community. Although they are quite different, the events in this section have some important characteristics in common:

- They are planned purposefully, with considerable attention to detail and logistics.

- Events reflect the values and expectations the community holds for everyday life in school.

- The faculty supports the event, and adults from all parts of the school community contribute and participate.

- Events are designed to include and engage all students.

As you read the examples in this section, notice how the purpose for each event drove its design, and how the schools' settings and values match what they chose to do. Then, when you are ready, use the discussion and planning questions at the end of this section to consider how your school might create a new all-school event or modify an existing one.

SECTION FOUR
Yearly Events

Fall Festival

Fall-themed activities replace
traditional Halloween festivities

PURPOSE

To include all
students, staff,
and families in a
seasonal celebration that everyone enjoys

At the end of Fall Festival, Ms. Boileau gathers her class of second graders in a circle and asks them to share one thing they remember about the day. Several children mention the hayride and the horses that pulled them; others recall square dancing at recess, the magician from the all-school assembly, and weighing pumpkins. One child shyly offers that he liked having his father come to school for lunch; others chime in and say they liked the picnic, too. When everyone has had a chance to share, Ms. Boileau wraps things up, saying, "We sure made a lot of good memories today!"

Eleanor Roosevelt Elementary School's annual Fall Festival combines classroom and whole-school activities in a day devoted to learning and fun. The event, which is held at the end of October, brings many parents into the school as volunteers and lunchtime guests. Although this all-school tradition was originally conceived as an alternative to Halloween festivities, in the years since it started, it has become part of Eleanor Roosevelt's school culture in its own right. "Today, no one misses the Halloween parade, or even asks about it," says principal Robert Wurst.

Mr. Wurst recalls noticing a dip in attendance on Halloween about a decade ago. Eleanor Roosevelt's students come from a variety of cultural and religious backgrounds, and some don't celebrate Halloween. It was apparent that some families were keeping their children home because the school day's events revolved around Halloween parties and an all-school costume parade.

Also, despite rules to the contrary, each Halloween some students came to school with faces painted and hair colored, and every year some children wore costumes in

---

Eleanor Roosevelt Elementary School, Morrisville, Pennsylvania
suburban; public ▪ K–5 ▪ 520 students ▪ 25 classrooms ▪ 8% of students receive free or reduced-price lunch

the parade that staff felt were inappropriately scary or violent. When Mr. Wurst discussed his concerns with the faculty, most of them agreed that the school's way of observing Halloween no longer seemed to fit the sort of school community they wanted to be.

When school staff explained the situation to the leaders of the school's PTO, they decided to collaborate on designing an event with an autumn theme that would be appealing and positive for the whole school community. The result was Fall Festival, which begins each year with a few schoolwide activities that build enthusiasm and set the stage before the day of the event. For instance, each class makes a scarecrow and displays it outside their classroom, and the PTO organizes contests that invite everyone in the school to guess the weight of a huge pumpkin and the number of candy corns in a jar.

On the day of Fall Festival, each class goes on a horse-drawn hayride on school grounds and the whole school comes together for an assembly. Many classes do seasonally-themed activities throughout the day, including reading and writing stories with an autumn setting, going on fall nature walks, and estimating and checking the weight of pumpkins. A highlight of the day is a picnic lunch outside, which many parents attend. Square dancing, which the children have learned in physical education class, is the main activity at recess. The day ends with each class gathering in their own room for games and fall food such as apples, popcorn, and gingersnaps.

Several groups share responsibility for planning Fall Festival. The PTO organizes schoolwide activities and recruits volunteers. Teachers plan their classroom activities and work with homeroom parents to organize the games and food at the end of the day. The principal schedules the hayrides and assembly, and the cafeteria provides bag lunches. "The way it all comes together really feels like a shared experience," says Mr. Wurst.

BENEFITS

Eleanor Roosevelt's Fall Festival has achieved its goal of creating an inclusive experience of fun and belonging for all of the school's students and families. Student attendance is strong for the day, and many parents come to the school to join their children for lunch. Teachers and the principal report that integrated classroom activities make Fall Festival a productive learning day, and that the day's special events successfully build schoolwide community.

Principal Robert Wurst emphasizes that by replacing an outdated tradition with a new one, Eleanor Roosevelt Elementary School aligned its practice with its beliefs. "We believe that all children should be included in all-school activities, and Fall Festival accomplishes that successfully."

Build support before changing traditions
"Changing long-held traditions is not easy. Move slowly, build consensus, and explain your reasons," says Mr. Wurst. "Don't give up if you believe what you're doing is right for the children." Even though staff and leaders of the Eleanor Roosevelt PTO supported ending the Halloween parade, some parents protested the change at first. They came to support the shift, though, after Mr. Wurst explained the reasoning behind it at an open meeting, and when the discussion that followed made it clear that a majority of the school's families supported discontinuation of the Halloween events.

Design it to engage everyone The Fall Festival includes a variety of activities, which helps ensure that the day has some element that appeals to each person who participates. The mix of inside and outside, grade level and whole school, and physical and intellectual challenges keeps things lively and interesting for students of all ages, abilities, and backgrounds.

Get help from volunteers This event involves many parent volunteers. To recruit them, the PTO sends a letter to parents early in the school year describing what the day will involve and asking parents to sign up to "join in the fun." Parents who respond indicate when they are available. Then they are matched with tasks that allow them to contribute meaningfully and manageably, in accordance with their schedules.

"Changing long-held traditions is not easy. Move slowly, build consensus, and explain your reasons."

Winter Carnival

An annual event focused on local
winter sports and activities

PURPOSE

To provide students
with a chance to
experience their
local community's
natural and recre-
ational assets

On Winter Carnival day, teacher Mary Beth DiMarco and thirty students aged five to eleven arrive at the frozen farm pond where they'll be ice fishing. They're greeted by a half-dozen volunteers who'd arrived earlier to drill holes in the ice and lay out equipment. Students who brought their own fishing gear start to set up, while the adults take charge of orienting the others. Before long, the first flag goes up, signaling a possible catch, and everyone rushes over to see what will come up when the line is pulled in.

Each February, Southern Aroostook Community School's teachers and staff, aided by many family and community volunteers, organize a day of winter activities for the 180 elementary students at this school in rural Maine. On the school's grounds and at a variety of locations in the community, mixed-age groups ice fish, ride snowmobiles, ski, ice skate, sled, snowshoe, build snow forts, and create snow sculptures. As Mary Beth DiMarco, the second grade teacher who organizes the ice fishing activity, explains, "It's a celebration of winter and what we can do here in our own community."

Grades K–5 participate in Winter Carnival, which is usually held on the last day before midwinter vacation begins. In January, staff members sign up to lead activities and begin making specific arrangements for their group. For example, Ms. DiMarco gets permission for her group to fish on a local pond that's been stocked with trout. In the meantime, Greg Bagley, the principal, arranges bus transportation for groups that will travel and orders lunches.

A few weeks before the event, children are asked to select the activity they'll try for the day. They indicate their first, second, and third choices on a permission form that lists the year's options and includes space for family members to sign up to vol-

Southern Aroostook Community School, Dyer Brook, Maine

rural; public ▪ K–12 ▪ 420 students total ▪ 12 elementary classrooms ▪ 56% of students receive free or reduced-price lunch
▪ school serves students from six communities

unteer. When the forms are distributed in school, teachers encourage the children to make thoughtful choices by considering what might be fun and hard about each activity, and to think about whether they want to try something they don't usually get to do. Since the permission slip must be signed by a parent or guardian, families also guide children's choices. The completed permission slips are returned to the elementary division secretary, who organizes the groups.

"We try to give everyone their first choice," says Mr. Bagley, "but for activities where the number of slots is very limited, such as snowmobiling, children who don't ordinarily have access to the activity get priority." Some children sign up for the same activity year after year, which has its own benefits. Ms. DiMarco notes that her group always includes some students who have prior experience with ice fishing. "Choosing this activity gives them a chance to be experts for the day. Some of them are children who don't have many chances to feel like an expert in school."

On the afternoon before Winter Carnival, groups gather in the classroom of the teacher who will lead their activity to go over rules and expectations. "We talk about my expectations and theirs," says Ms. DiMarco. In about thirty minutes she and the students cover everything from what to wear and who's bringing their own equipment, to thinking together about what will help ensure that everyone in the group has a good experience. This meeting sets the stage for a successful outing on many levels: information is conveyed, people in the group start getting to know one another, and excitement for the next day begins to build.

On the day of Winter Carnival, groups leave for their activities on a staggered schedule, so the school building gradually empties out as groups are called. Children start the day in their homerooms, moving to the classroom of their teacher for the day when their homeroom teacher's group departs. Teachers plan informal activities that are suitable for a mix of ages and easy to drop in on for this transition time.

Each group is joined by volunteers who are parents, grandparents, or community members with a connection to the activity. For the ice fishing group, these adult helpers bring equipment, build a fire for roasting hotdogs at lunch, and help each child get situated at his or her own fishing hole. "I definitely couldn't do it without them," says Ms. DiMarco.

At the end of the day, children and teachers return gradually, and the school fills back up. The ice fishing group goes first to Ms. DiMarco's classroom, and then disperses to their own homerooms as their teachers return. Teachers and students swap stories about the adventures they had, and when dismissal time comes, everyone heads off for midwinter break full of ideas for wintertime fun.

When dismissal time comes, everyone heads off for midwinter break full of ideas for wintertime fun.

Winter Carnival is Friday, February 16

Complete, sign, and return this form by **Wednesday, February 7th.**

Student Name: _____

EVENTS - Choose a 1st, 2nd, and 3rd choice.

At school:

____ Snowshoeing - We have some snowshoes. Bring your own if possible.

____ Cross Country Skiing - We have a limited number of skis. Use your own equipment if you'd like.

____ Snow Forts

____ Sliding - If you have a sled, please bring it.

Note: We are trying to secure a couple of snowmobiles to give rides to children who do activities here at school.

Away from school:

____ Ice Fishing - Lunch is provided.

____ Downhill Skiing/Snowboarding at Big Rock (Grade 2 and up) - Bring lunch money or a bag lunch.

____ Ice Skating at the Houlton Ice Arena - Some skates available. Bring your own if possible. Bring lunch money or a bag lunch.

____ Snowmobiling - To do this you must not have other opportunities to ride a snowmobile. Lunch is provided.

Permission Slip

I give my child, _____ , permission to participate in the above Winter Carnival activities on Friday, February 16th.

_____   _____
Signature   Date

Please check what you would be willing to help with on Friday, February 16th.

__ Snow Forts	__ Downhill Skiing/Snowboarding
__ Sliding	__ Ice Skating
__ Snowshoeing	__ Ice Fishing
__ Snowmobiling	__ Cross Country Skiing

_____
Your Name

Combination sign-up sheet and permission slip for Winter Carnival

Winter Carnival provides opportunities for learning that differ from those that students have on ordinary school days. "We feel that learning can take place in many areas," says Mr. Bagley. On this day, children interact with adults and each other outside of their classrooms, and they have a chance to reveal skills and talents that may not be evident in school. Also, because children of all ages participate in most of the activities, the day provides older and more experienced children with chances to be leaders.

This outing was deliberately conceived to connect children with their local community's natural and recreational assets. Mr. Bagley explains, "We live in a place where there are all these wonderful activities around—yet many of our students do not have the opportunity to engage in them." The school and community organizations collaborate to make the event affordable for all; most equipment and all transportation is free of cost to students, and lunch is provided for many activities.

Perhaps most importantly, Winter Carnival celebrates and sustains the strong sense of school community that Southern Aroostook has built over many years. It's a challenge to organize, but it's a highlight of the year for school families, community members, students, and staff. In the ten years since it started, the pool of volunteers has come to include a number of adults who continue to help out even though their children are no longer in elementary school. The focus on sporting activities brings in some volunteers who don't turn out as readily for other school events.

For teachers and students, connections made at Winter Carnival can endure for years. Ms. DiMarco notes that some of the children who ice fish with her become "my ice fishing buddies. I may never have them in my class, but when we see each other in the hallways, we know each other from that day."

KEYS TO SUCCESS

Designed to be inclusive This all-school outing is carefully designed to offer children a wide choice of safe and fun experiences. "We don't want to exclude anyone," says Mr. Bagley, explaining that they make sure the activities offered are age appropriate, that some have an indoor component (such as ice skating at a local rink), and that some take place on the school grounds. Winter Carnival takes place within the time constraints of an ordinary school day and is scheduled for a time of year when a day of fun is welcomed by all.

Responsibility distributed among staff An event of this scale involves coordinated effort from staff throughout the school. The advance preparation is divided among teachers, administrators, and staff; everyone takes responsibility for a clearly defined

> Planning for this event has gotten easier over time because experienced volunteers now do much more.

part. Mary Beth DiMarco also notes that the planning for this event has gotten easier over time because experienced volunteers now do much more.

Lots of volunteer and community support
Volunteer help and other community support for this event are vital to its success. Many volunteers return year after year and contribute not just experience, but equipment and supplies. The teachers who lead Winter Carnival activities coordinate with their volunteers by contacting each of them ahead of time to talk about how they will help. Community organizations donate goods, services, and access to venues.

Preparation for students Finally, the time the school invests in preparing students is an important part of what makes this day go well. The discussion about expectations that takes place the afternoon before Winter Carnival is part of this, but Greg Bagley and Mary Beth DiMarco both say the preparation actually starts long before that. Because at Southern Aroostook teachers all use the same positive approach to discipline, it's easy for them to communicate with students of all ages. "The children understand the rules," says Mr. Bagley, "and when they are outside the school they carry the rules with them." He notes proudly that there's never been a serious discipline problem in all the years they've held Winter Carnival.

Park Day

An annual spontaneous celebration
of outdoor fun

PURPOSE

To provide
students of all
ages with an
opportunity
to enjoy self-
directed time
outdoors

W*hen Keesha, a fourth grader, jumps out after her turn at double dutch and looks around, she can hardly believe the scene around her. The whole school is outside! Kids are playing street hockey on the tennis court, kickball on the small field, and investigating anthills near the trees. Darnell, her first grade cousin, is waving to her from the swings. Nearby, her teacher from last year is chatting with a kindergarten teacher while keeping an eye on some little kids playing in the sandbox. Keesha says good-bye to the double dutch group and heads over to say hello.*

Park Day is a much-loved annual tradition at Wissahickon Charter School (WCS), which serves students from throughout Philadelphia in a building located in an inner city industrial zone. Teachers and students use a nearby park for recess and as a field study site for classroom projects, but in general the students have few opportunities, during school or at home, to spend large amounts of time playing outside. After reading about a rural school's tradition of an all-school hike, WCS staff were inspired to create an opportunity for their students to enjoy what Dean of Faculty Kate O'Shea calls "a large chunk of self-directed time in the outdoors."

School staff schedule and plan each year's Park Day secretly, so that from the students' point-of-view, it's an impromptu celebration; one morning, teachers simply announce that it's Park Day at Morning Meeting, and everyone heads to the park soon afterwards. Classes travel together to an area far beyond the part of the park they usually use, circling up as they arrive. With their teacher and an administrator, they review established schoolwide outdoor rules, such as "Things that are alive must stay alive" and "Stay within sight of an adult at all times" and are shown where

---

Wissahickon Charter School, Philadelphia, Pennsylvania
urban; public charter ▪ K–8 ▪ 425 students ▪ 18 classrooms ▪ 89% of students receive free or reduced-price lunch
▪ school's focus is on environmental and peace education

Playing together brings joy to the school. Fourth graders play basketball with eighth graders, seventh graders help out kindergartners, and all ages play cooperative games together.

the school nurse, water fountains, and time-out area for the day are located. They're also introduced to the sound of the bell that will ring at lunchtime.

Once that orientation is complete, students are free to choose among adult-supervised activities such as tag, street hockey, basketball, kickball, or nature drawing, or to do something else on their own, such as organize a game, play with friends, explore, or try out the playground equipment. Children move between activities at their own pace for several hours before the bell rings to call them back together for a picnic lunch. Afterwards, the whole school assembles for a picture on a hillside, and then classes return to the school building.

Park Day is planned by a faculty committee—the Park Day Task Force. They choose the date (usually an early dismissal day in late April, around Arbor Day), arrange for the cafeteria to provide box lunches, and coordinate the activities. Using a map, they divide the park into zones and arrange adult supervision for specific areas and activities. Some years, they've organized supplementary activities such as tree-plantings and classroom read-alouds on environmental topics.

BENEFITS

Kate O'Shea says "students and staff look forward to this day and enjoy it to its fullest." Playing together brings joy to the school. Students mingle across different grade levels: fourth graders play basketball with eighth graders, seventh graders help out kindergartners, and all ages play cooperative games together. Staff members have a chance to interact with each other and with many students.

Park Day is designed to give WCS students freedom to choose how they will use their time. This student-directed approach successfully addresses the concern that originally inspired staff at the school to create Park Day—that children needed more free choice time in the outdoors. Ms. O'Shea recalls that six years ago when they planned the first Park Day, the task force briefly considered creating activity stations and assigning the children to groups. "But we saw that it would be an organizational nightmare, so we tried to find a simpler approach. What we settled on is much truer to our goals for the event."

KEYS TO SUCCESS

Careful planning and supervision The Park Day Task Force does a lot of advance planning to create an experience that allows students freedom while keeping them safe. The schedule for the day is carefully choreographed to include many appealing options for activities, and every area of the park is supervised. Kindergarten teachers don't supervise specific areas; instead they keep watch over the younger children. One staff member is assigned specifically to help students who need to calm down.

A schoolwide approach to discipline For Wissahickon Charter School, being able to hold a successful Park Day affirms the value of having a schoolwide approach to discipline. They can stage an event that involves taking over 400 people outside for hours of free play because in the classroom, all of the teachers use a similar approach to discipline. All students have participated in making classroom rules that travel with them to the park, and they have all learned strategies for practicing self-control that can be used in an outdoor setting, such as going to a designated time-out area to regain composure.

Park rules already in place Although Park Day takes place in an area of the park that is beyond the reach of everyday excursions, Wissahickon students are accustomed to working and learning outdoors, and staff and students have clear expectations for appropriate behavior in an outdoor setting. By April, when Park Day takes place, students have had plenty of practice following the school's outdoor and classroom rules, so a quick reminder during the orientation is all that most students need.

Sixth Grade Promotion

Personalized recognition for each student moving on to middle school

On the night of Maddux Elementary School's recognition ceremony, over 100 sixth graders cross the stage one by one before an audience of their families and teachers. The audience listens attentively after each name is called, holding their applause as the principal reads a complimentary phrase describing that student:

"Nina DiNicola, who set an example for others with her enthusiasm for science."

"Simon Weber, who had a smile for everyone."

"Stella Percival, who increased her personal best at the long jump by ten inches this year."

The phrases are selected from positive comments written by the children's present and former teachers and collected on a special card for each child. When the evening is over, each child is given his or her card to keep. This tradition involves teachers from all grade levels in providing a joyous send-off to every sixth grader. It has been a part of how the school year ends at Maddux for almost two decades.

The process starts each year in early March, when principal Stephen Troehler visits the sixth grade classrooms and hands out a large note card to each child. The children write their name at the top of the card, followed by a sentence describing a favorite memory of their time at Maddux. They write about activities, friends, and accomplishments. "I read all of their comments," says Mr. Troehler. "It's a way for me to find out which experiences have been most important to the students, and which school traditions should be continued."

Maddux Elementary School, Cincinnati, Ohio
suburban; public ■ K–6 ■ 658 students ■ 26 classrooms

Next, the cards are distributed to teachers. Each sixth grade teacher writes a positive comment on the card of every student in her or his class, and then passes the cards on to the art, music, and gym teachers. Those teachers add notes for students they want to compliment, and then they pass the cards on to teachers in descending order from grade five through kindergarten.

A staff listing travels with every card, and teachers check their names off before handing the card to another teacher. Each student's card circulates until it contains four comments. Completed cards are returned to the principal, who then adds his own note.

From the collection of comments for each child, the principal selects one to read aloud at the recognition ceremony. Considerations include what the student would appreciate most and what would be easy to understand when read aloud. If what the child wrote is powerful, the principal might choose to read that comment.

After the ceremony, each child's card is presented to the student, who can now read all the comments and see who wrote them. Diane Method, the retired Maddux principal who started the tradition, says students "really cherish their cards. In all the bustle of the end of the school year, those cards were not lost or left behind. In sixteen years, I never found one dropped on the floor."

"Students really cherish their cards. In all the bustle of the end of the school year, those cards were not lost or left behind."

BENEFITS

This tradition engages teachers from throughout the school in reflecting on sixth graders' accomplishments, reinforcing the idea that all adults in the school are involved in children's growth during their elementary years. In addition, even though space constraints limit attendance at the recognition ceremony to sixth graders, their families, and sixth grade teachers, the note card tradition brings the voices of many teachers onto the stage, making the ceremony feel more like a schoolwide event.

This tradition also makes it possible for each sixth grader in a group of 100 or more to enjoy a moment of meaningful public acclaim as he or she walks across the stage at the recognition ceremony. Every sixth grader receives the same amount of attention, and for the audience, hearing all the different comments helps them appreciate the diversity of strengths among the students and the rich learning they experienced during their elementary years.

Comments are meaningful and well deserved For this activity to be meaningful, the comments teachers write about each child have to be genuine and well deserved. At Maddux, the children's sixth grade year includes many opportunities for them to contribute to the school as leaders, role models, and helpers. As a result, the school community has many opportunities to see them in a positive light. Teachers write about special times and strengths they truly observed in the students.

Teachers have shared understanding about appropriate comments Ms. Method recalls that when Maddux first launched this tradition, the staff talked at faculty meetings about what sorts of comments would be appropriate for the cards. They noted that these cards were not the place for "needs improvement" comments, but rather for remarks about a laudable characteristic or something positive the child had done. For children for whom it was hard to think of a general comment, staff agreed to think of one particular shining moment for the child and write about that. Over the years, with this shared understanding established, there has been less need for discussion. Nowadays new faculty members are still introduced to the process, but more informally.

Number of comments per child is limited In the first year, the number of comments for each child was not limited, and some students' cards were crammed full, while others were not. This caused problems when cards were handed back to the students, because the children inevitably focused on who got more. To prevent bad feelings, the school established a guideline of four comments per child. When the temptation to compare is removed, each child is freed to savor his or her compliments—and to enjoy the good feeling that comes from knowing that everyone in the grade had positives worth recognizing.

Student of the Year

Aligning a community tradition with school values

PURPOSE

To make an award competition into an opportunity for schoolwide learning, reflection, and celebration

During Regional Multicultural Magnet School's Moving-On Day ceremony, the school's director honors the finalists for "Student of the Year" by reading excerpts from nomination essays written by their classmates:

"Always fair, he never teases, even if he has to be against his friends ..."

"She has the power to encourage people to be their very best ..."

"Someone people look up to. She uses her imagination to solve problems ..."

"He helps classmates learn English, and he learns Spanish from them ..."

Nominating peers for the local Rotary Club's Student of the Year award is a prominent end-of-the-year activity for fifth graders at Regional Multicultural Magnet School (RMMS). During the final weeks of school, the students, with guidance from the school director and their teachers, think and write about how their classmates embody the values expressed in the school's mission statement. This peer nomination process allows RMMS to participate in a community tradition in a manner that feels true to the school's values, and at the same time, provides students with a meaningful opportunity to apply their essay writing skills.

A community tradition

The idea of giving one outgoing student a year-end award was first proposed to RMMS about ten years ago by the local Rotary Club. The idea presented some problems, recalls then school director Richard Spindler-Virgin. "Our school does very

---

Regional Multicultural Magnet School, New London, Connecticut
urban; public magnet ▪ K–5 ▪ 500 students ▪ 28 classrooms ▪ 38% of students receive free or reduced-price lunch
▪ school includes students from twelve rural, suburban, and urban districts

> The process is kicked off in mid-May by gathering all the fifth graders to discuss the school's mission statement and the nomination process.

little that is individually competitive," he explains. Instead, the school emphasizes "cooperation, compassion, and working together in community. These are all things that foster the individual's responsibility to the group and can be in opposition to one person getting recognized." As a result, until then the school had purposefully avoided giving traditional individual awards. Instead, the focus at the end of the year was on having students share reflections on their learning and accomplishments. When recognition was given, it was for the accomplishments of groups, such as the choral ensemble.

However, in part because the award was a community-wide tradition (the Rotary Club recognizes a Student of the Year from each local elementary school), RMMS staff decided it was important to participate. So they designed a selection process that is consistent with RMMS's values and that includes all of the fifth graders in deciding who receives the award.

Discussing the mission statement

Each year the process begins in mid-May when the school's director gathers all the fifth graders, about sixty students, to discuss the school's mission statement and the nomination process. The director asks students to consider each of the four elements of the mission statement: respecting cultural diversity; empowering all learners; developing compassionate people; and making positive changes in society. Next, students name ways a person might demonstrate each element. Ideas typically include such actions as "show an interest in other people's traditions," "help someone who doesn't understand," "be understanding of mistakes," and "stand up for someone being bullied."

Writing nomination essays

Later, students refer to the list of examples as they plan and write an essay about a classmate who, in their opinion, did most of those things most of the time during their years at RMMS. Students can write about themselves if they aren't comfortable nominating a peer, or if they feel they best embody the mission of the school.

They are encouraged to base their decisions on evidence, not popularity. They are also advised to keep their choices secret to avoid hurt feelings.

The writing of the essays is completed as a classroom activity. Teachers instruct students to structure their nomination essays the same way they've learned to structure other types of expository writing: using paragraphs, each containing a main idea supported by evidence and good detail. Mr. Spindler-Virgin notes that this is "a great writing prompt. The topic is something the children can relate to. They know that if they do a good job, the person they are nominating has a chance to win."

Determining the finalists and winner

When the essays are completed, the director and teachers read them all. They consider the quality of evidence offered for the handful of students who receive numerous (typically five or more) nominations and choose the finalists. The director writes a letter to the families of each of those children, including quotes from the essays about their child. All of the finalists are recognized during RMMS's Moving-On Day ceremony, which is attended by the whole school as well as by fifth graders' families.

Staff members identify one child among the finalists who stands out as having a broader and deeper sense of the mission, and this child is named Student of the Year. The Student of the Year is individually recognized at a luncheon hosted by the Rotary Club.

"That part is an honor for that child, but for everyone else in the school, the emphasis is more on the process and the Moving-On ceremony, where we read excerpts from the nomination essays and recognize all the finalists," says former director, Sally Myers. Using a peer-nomination process and making the award part of the larger farewell program puts the award in context and helps all students feel ownership of it, she explains.

BENEFITS

Connecting the Student of the Year award to the school's mission creates an opportunity for many members of the RMMS community to reflect on what it means to live up to those standards. The nominating process deepens fifth grade students' understanding of the mission statement and enables them to connect the mission directly with their personal lives. Also, over the years, as the award has become a central part of Moving-On Day, hearing excerpts from the nomination essays has raised younger students' awareness of the mission as well.

The peer nomination process engages the whole fifth grade in thinking about who among them deserves to receive the award, which can increase its significance for those who are recognized. At least one past recipient said the award meant more to her because it came from her peers, whom she felt knew her better than the teachers did.

The process RMMS uses to select its Student of the Year provides an opportunity for teachers and students to end the year on a positive note. Mr. Spindler-Virgin recalls that from the first year, "having students do this kind of exercise, where they have the opportunity to write in a positive way about other students, was really rewarding. To have people saying all these wonderful things countered some of the more frenzied stuff that happens at the end of the year. What a breath of fresh air it was!"

KEYS TO SUCCESS

The task builds on common knowledge and beliefs Tying the Student of the Year award to the RMMS mission works because RMMS is truly a mission-driven school. When the director sits down with the fifth graders at the end of the school year to talk about the mission, it's not the first time they've read or thought about it. The vision of school as a cooperative, respectful community made up of caring people is kept in the consciousness of students, staff, and families throughout the year, and it guides much of the day-to-day decision making at this school.

The task builds on familiar skills The writing component of the process is successful because it asks students to apply expository writing skills they've already learned. All of the steps—from brainstorming examples, to choosing main ideas and supporting evidence, to organizing paragraphs—are familiar to students. As a result, students write nominations that are well argued and convincing, and they experience firsthand the persuasive power of skills they've acquired in school.

Students are supported in making good decisions Although students decide whom to nominate, the school's director and teachers help them make thoughtful, evidence-based choices. For example, when Ms. Myers met with the fifth graders, she focused first on developing shared understanding of the mission by asking them to generate a long list of concrete, anonymous examples. Then, before the students began working on their nomination essays, she explicitly addressed issues of popularity and hurt feelings, stating clear expectations and giving advice about how to prevent problems. The fifth grade teachers also watch for trouble and quickly address any issues that come up. They say that due to the nature of the activity and the ways in which students are prepared for it, fifth graders rarely have problems choosing a peer to be Student of the Year or providing evidence for their choice.

Discussion and Planning Questions

These questions are intended for use by groups such as school leadership teams, parent-teacher partnerships, and cross-grade committees who have chosen to work together on building schoolwide community.

The suggestions on these pages are intended to help guide your group through the process of considering, planning, and holding special events at your school.

Before deciding on a specific event:

Envision Imagine what a really great all-school event would be like at your school.

- What could you do?

- Where might you go?

- What sort of experience would be especially rewarding? To whom?

Be purposeful Make sure you can explain what the school community hopes to gain from holding the event.

- Who will benefit and how?

- What are your goals?

- What results do you expect?

Take stock Think about the everyday procedures and skills that need to be in place for the event to go smoothly. Make a plan for building these skills ahead of time in classroom or smaller groups.

- What do students and staff know how to do already?

- What needs to be taught?

- To whom? By whom?

Once you have selected an event:

Consider logistics Work out practical details ahead of time.

- When will the event take place?

- If the event is off-site, how will participants get there and back?

- How long will it take, including travel time?

- Will you need to provide lunch and/or snacks?

- When will participants have access to restrooms?

- How much adult supervision will students need?

- How will staff be distributed?

- What will volunteers do?

- How will you maintain contact with the school while off-site?

- What is your plan for communicating in the event of an emergency?

- How will the event begin? How will it end?

- How will transitions be handled?

- What other details do you need to consider ahead of time?

Introduce the project Make sure that everyone involved understands the plan and goals for the day

- How will you introduce it to students?

- How will you inform others, including school staff, students' families, and the local community, about the event?

Recruit and prepare volunteers Ask for help well in advance and give volunteers specific, meaningful tasks.

- How will you get the word out to potential volunteers?

- Who will supervise their work? What can volunteers do to help this event?

- What parts of this event should they not be responsible for?

Prepare students Work on building the new skills that students need specifically for the event.

- What do students need to think about and learn to do ahead of time?

- When and how will the preparation take place?

Afterwards:

Evaluate Take time to reflect on how it went. Think about what could be improved, but be sure to notice and celebrate what went well, too.

- Did it go as you expected?

- Were there any surprises?

- What went well?

- What could make this go better next time?

Remain purposeful As you think about next time, consider your original reasons for holding this event.

- Did the event accomplish the purpose you originally set?

- Has your purpose changed? Is it time to set different goals?

Involving Families

Strong connections between home and school increase children's chances for success. Schools forge these connections by involving families in their children's education: listening to their insights; informing them about the school's approach to teaching and learning; inviting them to visit and volunteer; offering them ideas for helping their children with schoolwork; and welcoming them to contribute to school programs and policies.

Including families can be a challenge because of schedules, transportation, and child-care issues. Guarded attitudes and misperceptions—on the part of families toward school, and on the part of school toward families—can also be obstacles. But schools and families can arrive at a trusting relationship. This trust has to be deliberately built. Often the key is to proceed slowly and purposefully.

Initial activities might be primarily social, such as game nights, ice cream socials, and movie nights, all focused on having fun while allowing families to become familiar with the school building and staff, and staff to become familiar with families' lives and interests. Once everyone feels more comfortable with each other in the school environment, families may be more likely to volunteer in classrooms or participate in more educational activities such as family literacy and math nights. School staff, meanwhile, will be better able to design family involvement opportunities to suit families' needs and interests.

In this section, you'll read about some of the ways six schools have reached out to families. Their stories share characteristics that apply generally to efforts to include families in schoolwide community:

- All children and their families are welcomed and valued.

- Events and activities are participatory, interactive, and include opportunities to socialize.

- Family work schedules and family time are respected.

As you read this section, notice how each event was developed purposefully, and how each helps build and strengthen community. Think about ways your school involves families already, and then use the discussion and planning questions at the end of the chapter to work on enhancing this element of community building at your school.

Walking Wednesdays

Students, parents, and teachers walk together during recess once a week

"Here you go, Tyler!"

Tyler takes the punchcard that tracks how many miles he's walked from a parent volunteer. He thanks her and steps aside to wait for Kai and Scott, the friends he likes to walk with.

Within minutes, Tyler, Kai, Scott, and nearly 150 other children and adults all have their punchcards in hand, and a parade of walkers has begun to make its way around the building. Children walk in small groups or alone, sometimes falling into step to chat with the teachers who are walking today. They wave at the adults posted at each corner of the course and pause to have their cards punched each time they complete a lap.

The Parent Teacher Organization coordinates Walking Wednesdays, a popular voluntary activity at Young School. Each Wednesday, adult volunteers mark out the course around the building and supervise walkers during two sessions of lunchtime recess. Students and teachers who choose to walk are joined by younger siblings, parents, and grandparents who visit the school for this twenty minute activity.

The PTO uses Feeling Good Mileage Club® materials to keep track of how many miles each child, each class, and the whole school walks during the year. Significant milestones are celebrated with hallway displays and during Young's monthly all-school meeting. The total number of miles walked by everyone is calculated and mapped to a destination: one year the distance the whole school walked was equivalent to a

---

Young School, Saco, Maine
suburban; public ▪ K–2 ▪ 295 students ▪ 11 classrooms ▪ 5% of students receive free or reduced-price lunch

loop that went up to the top of Mt. Katahdin in Maine, over to Ben and Jerry's ice cream factory in Vermont, and back to the school; another year, they walked enough miles to make it to the Statue of Liberty.

BENEFITS

The children look forward to walking and most choose to walk for at least part of each Wednesday recess. Principal Peter Harrison says that for students who do not enjoy games or using the playground equipment, this provides an alternative way to exercise. "We hope it will build lifelong habits around fitness, especially for children who aren't athletically inclined."

The program also creates a low-key opportunity for families to get involved with the school, both as organizers and participants. It gives younger siblings a preview of what school will be like, and provides parents and grandparents a chance to spend informal time with children outside. Many family members participate regularly.

Walking Wednesdays Word Problems

1. *In April, Ms. Collins' class walked 9 miles, Ms. Pulsifer's class walked 7 miles, and Ms. Cartwright's class walked 10 miles. How many miles did these three classes walk in all?*

2. *Young School in Saco, Maine is 306 miles from the Statue of Liberty in New York.*

   a. *How many miles is the round trip (going there and coming back)?*

   b. *So far this year, our school has walked 427 miles on Walking Wednesdays. How many more miles are needed to get us to the Statue of Liberty and back?*

Sample math problems using Walking Wednesdays data

Teachers use the records of miles walked to make curriculum connections. The data is used in math problems, graphs, and mapping exercises. Children use punchcards to track their individual mileage and receive a footprint-shaped certificate each time they fill up a card. These footprints are displayed in school hallways, and as they accumulate they provide a visual of how the whole school's miles are adding up that even the youngest students can appreciate.

KEYS TO SUCCESS

Rules are taught and enforced consistently Young School has developed school-wide rules for recess, and at the beginning of each year teachers teach and review these guidelines. Having these universal rules in place in addition to specific guidelines for the event makes Walking Wednesdays go more smoothly. Before Walking Wednesdays begin for the year, each class reviews the boundaries of the walking course, and practices walking and skipping around it.

Adult volunteers have clear roles At Young School, Walking Wednesdays logistics are managed by a group of parent volunteers who run the activity in parallel with regular recess. Staff have playground duty at this time, just as they do on other days. The Walking Wednesday parent volunteers focus only on the walkers, while staff watch over the whole playground.

Competition is not emphasized Although children are naturally interested in comparing their punchcards and seeing who's gone farthest, the school encourages them to focus more on setting and reaching personal goals. One way they de-emphasize the competitive aspects of this activity is by making it truly voluntary. At Young, children genuinely choose whether to walk each Wednesday; they are not pressured to walk if they'd prefer to play a game or do something else at recess.

New Families Night

Starting with a warm welcome

Before school begins, Penn Valley Elementary School in Levittown, Pennsylvania holds "New Families Night" for students and families who are just joining the school. The purpose is to introduce the families to the school and to each other. On the night of the event, school staff and PTO members greet the families as they arrive and take their picture for a bulletin board display in the school's front lobby. Then families take part in a "get to know you" activity that encourages mixing and mingling. Next, the whole group gathers in a circle in the gym. Each family introduces itself by name, and the group choruses back, "Hello, _____ Family."

Afterwards the students and adult family members split up. The children participate in a modified version of a Morning Meeting, a routine that takes place daily in every classroom at Penn Valley. This introduction helps them get to know other new students and to learn a few greetings, activities, and songs. That way, when it's Morning Meeting time in their new classroom, they feel more comfortable because they know how the routine works. Meanwhile, their parents and guardians are meeting key people in the school—such as the reading specialist, nurse, guidance counselor, instructional support teacher, and principal—learning what each of them does, and how to contact them. This is also an opportunity for the school staff to begin getting to know the parents.

The evening ends with light refreshments and an opportunity for a tour. Families leave feeling welcomed and more knowledgeable about the school. School staff leave with more knowledge about the families, and new students arrive on the official first day already feeling that they belong.

Penn Valley Elementary School, Levittown, Pennsylvania
suburban; public ▪ K–5 ▪ 310 students ▪ 18 classrooms ▪ 5 self-contained special education classrooms

Involving
Families

123

Wissahickon Reads

A schoolwide reading initiative focused
on families reading together

O n the inaugural *Wissahickon Reads* night, 200 students and their families
traveled from room to room in the school to complete activities related to
George Selden's classic novel, A Cricket in Times Square. *At the science station they made detailed drawings of live crickets, and at the Reader's Theater center
they acted out scenes from the book. In other areas, mixed-age groups of students
wrote poetry, completed a "webquest" designed by the technology teacher, and
designed and built imaginary insects. Meanwhile, in the library, book discussions
unfolded on topics ranging from favorite parts of the novel to the stereotypical repre-
sentation of a Chinese character.*

Wissahickon Reads takes place once or twice a year at Wissahickon Charter
School. In this voluntary program, the school selects thematically-related books at
different reading levels and invites students and their families to read them together
at home. Four to six weeks later, the school hosts a celebratory evening of activities
related to the books. The program builds schoolwide community and strengthens the
school's connection with families. "Our goals for Wissahickon Reads are to get students reading, to involve parents in our instructional program, and to reinforce our
school's environmental mission," says Dean of Faculty Kate O'Shea.

A faculty committee called the Wissahickon Reads Task Force chooses the
books for each cycle of Wissahickon Reads, selecting high quality literature that
reflects the educational mission of the school. Once the books for the cycle are
announced, many teachers read the first chapters aloud to their classes to get the
children interested.

Wissahickon Charter School, Philadelphia, Pennsylvania
urban; public charter ▪ K–8 ▪ 425 students ▪ 18 classrooms ▪ 89% of students receive free or reduced-price lunch
▪ school's focus is on environmental and peace education

Copies of the chosen books are made widely available for families to buy or borrow. Adults or older siblings might read aloud with younger children, or family members might read independently. With their books, each family receives a bookmark containing suggestions for reading with children of different ages.

At the evening of activities that concludes each reading cycle, there are typically six or more learning stations, each created by a teacher from a different subject area in an effort to appeal to multiple intelligences. Activities at the learning stations are designed to be engaging for students in grades K–8 and to be completed in about twenty minutes each. Students and their family members sign in and move from station to station on their own, with the aid of bells that signal when twenty minutes have passed. The event, which takes about two hours, is fun and informal, with plenty of opportunities for parents to chat and for students to work and play in mixed-age groups.

> With their books, each family receives a bookmark containing suggestions for reading with children of different ages.

BENEFITS

Kate O'Shea recalls that "the first time we held the evening event, we had no idea what to expect. Out of 300 students in the school, over 200 and their family members attended the evening, and many students completed all six stations with glee." Since then, Wissahickon Reads has continued to be a popular schoolwide activity. The school has noticed more parent participation overall, improved reading test scores, and higher rates of students reporting that they enjoy reading.

The initiative has also proven to be a valuable venue for parent education. Through Wissahickon Reads, the school emphasizes the importance of reading at home and is able to provide tips for adults who aren't accustomed to reading with children. The book selections expose families to topics related to the school's environmental mission, and the range of interactive, multidisciplinary activities at the culminating event show families the instructional approach WCS uses during the school day.

Reading the same book, or books on a shared theme, also unifies the school in a special way. During Wissahickon Reads, students of all ages gain knowledge about a common topic they can talk about together. Because teachers from across the school participate, they, too, are brought closer together as colleagues. At the culminating event, learning stations grounded in different subject areas reinforce that reading skills are important for learning in all disciplines.

Committed team leadership Producing Wissahickon Reads requires a commitment of time and effort from teachers. At this school, where there is a culture of faculty working beyond their own classrooms, each teacher serves on a task force, and the Wissahickon Reads group is one such committee. The faculty members who choose to work on Wissahickon Reads therefore perceive this work as a job responsibility rather than an extra duty.

Thoughtful planning and improvements The task force's behind-the-scenes efforts are essential to the success of Wissahickon Reads. For instance, they search out books that will be meaningful and engaging for their students and their families. They've also improved the program over time: The first year, the whole school read the same book. But since then the school has shifted to focusing on themes such as "water," "mysteries," and "animal perspectives," which allows the committee to select books from a range of reading levels.

Promoting the program Understanding that the best program can flop without good publicity, the committee puts conscious effort into promoting each cycle of Wissahickon Reads. Their methods range from sending flyers home to launching "advertising campaigns" at school that use posters, contests, and special events to build interest.

Well prepared students Although the reading and activities for Wissahickon Reads take place mostly outside of regular school time, the skills and experience children gain in their classrooms play an important part in this program's success. Students are able to manage independent reading, participate productively in book discussions, and work with children of other ages in learning centers because they have practiced doing those things in school. Wissahickon Reads activities are fun variations on an approach to learning with which students are already familiar.

Authors' Day

An annual schoolwide celebration
of students as writers

PURPOSE

To celebrate students' accomplishments as writers by reading finished work to parents and other visitors

For Authors' Day, Julie Berry's kindergarten class has made a book called I Am Special. As two dozen visitors look on proudly, each kindergartner takes a turn sitting in the Authors' Chair to read the page he or she wrote and illustrated. At the end, when Ms. Berry closes the cover, the audience bursts into applause.

At Broad Brook Elementary School, each grade hosts an Authors' Day during a two week span in May. On that day, family members visit their children's classrooms to hear students read a piece of their writing from the year. Each hour-long gathering celebrates students' accomplishments and draws parents' attention to children's literacy skills as the summer is about to start. Holding a series of Authors' Days that involves all the classes builds schoolwide enthusiasm for writing and highlights students' shared experiences as authors, while affirming the importance of literacy to the Broad Brook community.

Broad Brook uses a writing process approach and writers workshops throughout the school, so students at all grade levels have experience writing and revising, sharing their work with classmates, and publishing polished, illustrated final versions. For Authors' Day, the youngest students generally create a class book, to which each child contributes a page. Students in first through fourth grades choose a piece of their writing from the year to publish and share.

Several weeks before Authors' Day, classroom teachers and Broad Brook's reading teacher, Kim Dessert, begin guiding students as they select and polish the writing they will present. They also provide students with opportunities to practice reading their work aloud so they will be able to do so fluently and confidently before an audience. In the meantime, parents receive information and the schedule for the year's Authors' Days in the school's weekly bulletin. Some classes also create and send home invitations.

On Authors' Day itself, classroom teachers greet visitors and begin the sharing by describing the process students used to produce their finished pieces. They also explain how the readings will work that day. In some classrooms, children read to the entire group of guests and classmates, while in others, teachers create small groups and several authors read at once. Either way, "The children feel special and proud of their accomplishments," says assistant principal Laura Foxx. "They love having an audience respond to their work."

After the readings, if time allows, children read other books one-on-one with guests before gathering for refreshments at a classroom authors' reception. At the end of the celebration, each child receives a small memento related to writing, such as a special pencil, pen, or sticker.

BENEFITS

The original goal of Authors' Day was to extend students' feeling of accomplishment about their writing by having them share it with a wider audience. Ten years since it was started, Authors' Day still achieves that goal, but it has also become a cherished tradition at Broad Brook. Almost all students have a parent or grandparent attend, so students read to packed classrooms. Ms. Foxx says that preparing for Authors' Day builds students' enthusiasm for writing, and that the day itself "is a celebration of our community and the work all students have accomplished."

Authors' Day bridges school and home by providing parents with a chance to learn about how their children are learning to write. Sometimes, the school gathers parents as they arrive for Authors' Day and uses the opportunity to show a video on how to do literacy activities with children at home. But most important is that Authors' Day offers a public opportunity to celebrate all students' accomplishments in this area.

KEYS TO SUCCESS

Authors' Day is integrated with curriculum Authors' Day is a natural extension of classroom practices that Broad Brook uses schoolwide. As Laura Foxx says, "If writers workshop is a meaningful part of classroom life throughout the year, an event like Authors' Day is much easier to organize and more likely to be a success." Students and teachers at Broad Brook have a year's worth of writing and workshop experience to draw on when preparing for Authors' Day.

Students and teachers have time to prepare Still, getting all the students in a class ready to share at the same time takes some coordination. Teachers may need extra help publishing student-authored books during the weeks before the event, and students will need time to practice reading aloud. Even though students have experience sharing writing with classmates, presenting their work at Authors' Day is a bit more formal, in part because the audience is larger and includes familiar and unfamiliar adults. Some Broad Brook teachers recommend having children practice by reading to an adult, pointing out that students tend to be better listeners on Authors' Day if they have not heard their classmates' stories before.

"The children feel special and proud of their accomplishments. They love having an audience respond to their work."

Event is planned with parents' needs in mind To make it possible for working parents to attend, a daytime event such as Authors' Day has to be brief, and families must have plenty of advance notice about the date. In its communications home about Authors' Day, Broad Brook provides details that help parents know what to expect, and the school makes every minute of the gathering count. By scheduling each grade level's Authors' Day on a different day, they simplify parking and make it possible for parents to visit different-aged children's classrooms.

Talent Days

A chance for every child to shine

At the University School of Nashville, Talent Days are an annual spring celebration held class-by-class in the music room. For a few weeks, the school welcomes a stream of visitors who come to cheer on students as they share a kaleidoscope of skills and interests. Children in grades 1–4 demonstrate talents such as magic, photography, cooking, writing, gymnastics, training pets, singing, and playing instruments before an enthusiastic audience of classmates, teachers, and family members.

Each class has its own Talent Day. By early spring, the children know each other well, and the music room has become a comfortable, safe-feeling environment. Every student who chooses to do so makes a three minute presentation. Children perform solo or with a companion. Skills that can't be presented in the classroom, such as roller skating, are shared via video or photographs.

Music teacher Doni Princehorn, who organizes Talent Days, says that she's seen children benefit in many ways from their Talent Day experiences. The event allows all students to be recognized, whether their special interest is in music or some other area, and sends a schoolwide message that students have skills and talents to share at every age.

University School of Nashville, Nashville, Tennessee
urban; independent ■ K–12 ■ 1000 students ■ 20 classrooms in grades K–4

Success Night

An annual celebration of all
students' accomplishments

PURPOSE

To engage the
whole school
community in
reflecting on stu-
dents' growth
and learning

*W*hen Kyle and his grandparents walk into the school on Success Night,
the hallways are buzzing with children and their families moving from
classroom to classroom. Kyle's grandmother catches sight of his second
grade teacher and waves.

*Kyle says they'll visit her room later. "First I'm going to show you what I've been
doing this year." And he steers them eagerly down the hallway to his fifth grade
classroom.*

Success Night, held on an evening in May, is the most popular family event of the
year at Summit Elementary School. Every student in the school participates by creating a public display highlighting his or her proudest accomplishments for the year;
on the night itself, hundreds of family members attend the celebration, which marks
a year of learning and growth for the whole school community.

Most families spend the first forty-five minutes of Success Night in their child's
classroom and then an equal amount of time visiting other areas of the school,
including a break for ice cream in the cafeteria. After the first half of the evening,
teachers leave their classrooms so they, too, can see the student work displayed
throughout the building. "The hallways and classrooms are just decorated to the
max," says kindergarten teacher Katie Geiger. "It's the end of the year, but it's so
clear that learning is still going on."

Although they all share the common goal of having students reflect on and represent their accomplishments from the year, classes at each grade level prepare for

> ## Welcome to Summit Success Night!
>
> ### Be sure to …
>
> ❈
>
> *Visit the "Guess Who" bulletin board in the hallway. Have your family try to find your riddle.*
>
> ❈
>
> *Check your mailbox. Someone has left something special for you there!*
>
> ❈
>
> *Show your family your animal report.*
>
> ❈
>
> *Visit the second grade classrooms (Rooms 204, 205, 206, and 207). Look for things that are the same and different from your first grade classroom.*
>
> ❈
>
> *Thank your family for coming and sharing in your success tonight!*

Itinerary for Success Night from a first grade classroom

Success Night differently. Teachers connect preparations to curriculum and current issues in their students' lives. For instance, Katie Geiger integrates her class's build up to Success Night with a year-end focus on preparing the children to transition to first grade and a full-length school day.

She begins the process by showing the children the pages where, back in September, they'd drawn pictures and dictated sentences describing their hopes for their kindergarten year. She says that at this age, the children's hopes for the year are usually quite simple and concrete. For instance, they might have said they hoped to have a class pet, or to hear lots of stories. Ms. Geiger asks students to think about whether they accomplished their goals. However, she explains, this exercise is about more than seeing if their hopes came true: "It also gets children thinking about how much they've grown. When I show them these and other samples of their work from earlier in the year, they can't believe how they used to do things."

At the end of this process, each child makes a poster highlighting something he or she feels especially proud of having done in kindergarten. These posters are displayed in the classroom on Success Night.

When visitors arrive on Success Night, Ms. Geiger provides each family with a list of things they might do together during the evening. Activities such as reading a favorite book, looking through journals, and admiring the posters all spotlight the students' accomplishments. Other tasks build excitement for first grade and provide reassurance that children will be able to make the transition successfully. For example, the children lead visitors to various locations—a first grade classroom, the art and music rooms, and the gym—to carry out tasks such as measuring objects like a stool, a cone, and a rhythm stick and then return to the kindergarten room with their measurements.

For older students, such as those in Lisa Courtney's fifth grade class, Success Night is the culmination of a reflective process that begins in April with preparation for state-wide testing. At first, teachers focus on reviewing academic topics covered in fifth grade; then, after testing is complete, they ask students to reflect on their growth and learning as individuals in four areas: academics, athletics, creative pursuits, and citizenship. Each fifth grader selects an accomplishment in one of those areas to describe in writing and support with evidence. Their essays and the accompanying evidence—such as certificates, notes from teachers, work samples, and objects—are displayed on their desks on Success Night.

By the end of fifth grade, most students and their families feel at home in the school and have lots of ideas about what they'd like to see and do on Success Night, so Ms. Courtney simply provides suggestions for an itinerary: she advises parents to look first at their child's work, followed by the work of his or her classmates, and then to visit other grade levels and specials teachers' rooms.

BENEFITS

Success Night not only provides parents, grandparents, and other family members with an opportunity to learn about children's individual accomplishments—it also increases families' sense of connection to the school as a whole. With teachers, students, and their families intermingled throughout the school, all learning about student accomplishments across grades, "it feels like a celebration of all of us," says Ms. Courtney.

Success Night also helps people in the school get to know each other better. By seeing students' displays in the hallways and reading students' reflections on their accomplishments in a variety of areas, teachers and classmates learn about children's talents, interests, news, and growth. Many classes make games for Success Night that build on this theme. For instance, first grade classes make posters with a question written on a flap ("Guess who got a baby brother this year?") which hides the child's picture and name. Another class makes "five important things to know about me" posters and invites visitors to guess which student made each one.

Finally, Success Night gives all students in the school an opportunity to shine before their families, teachers, and peers. At Summit, this event has replaced the traditional year-end awards ceremony, which singled some students out and left others unrecognized. Success Night is both a more inclusive and a more positive way to end the school year. Lisa Courtney explains, "With Success Night, students describe their achievements in their own words, and the focus is on celebrating growth and being proud, which applies to everyone."

KEYS TO SUCCESS

Reflective projects are customized by class Each teacher at Summit decides how her or his students will represent their learning on Success Night and guides the process so it's developmentally appropriate. Many classes collect work samples throughout the year in portfolios; these collections become resources for students as they reflect on their learning. For older students, the reflective work completed for Success Night is a direct extension of familiar classroom routines: for instance, each fifth grader makes a selection from his or her portfolio for a classroom display each month.

Special area teachers also have displays on Success Night. They display student products and processes from the year, and many people visit them. These teachers tend to use the first forty-five minutes (when almost all students and parents are in their homerooms) to travel through the building, see classroom displays, and touch base with students. They then return to their "home bases" for the second half of the evening, which is the time that most parents and students come to visit them.

Families understand how to navigate the event Success Night has an informal feel, with visitors moving through the school at their own pace. Summit staff emphasize that to make this work, parents have to know what to expect and what to do. Most teachers provide guidelines families can follow if they wish; in school beforehand, students practice being guides. Over the years, teachers have also learned some strategies for setting up classroom displays in ways that invite visitors to explore, such as leaving folders containing student work open, rather than closed.

Staff and parents collaborate and fine tune When Summit's first Success Night was held, it worked somewhat differently than it does today. For instance, Principal Kathy Marx recalls that when it first started, an awards ceremony was actually part of Success Night, and that it took a while for the school to move away from giving awards. Over several years, a committee that included teachers, administrators and parents reflected on the school's goals for the end of the school year and fine tuned year-end events accordingly. The result, ten years later, is an all-school tradition that celebrates all students and is universally beloved.

Discussion and Planning Questions

These questions are intended for use by groups such as school leadership teams, parent-teacher partnerships, and cross-grade committees who have chosen to work together on building schoolwide community.

The suggestions on these pages are intended to help guide your group through the process of considering, planning, and hosting activities and events that involve students' families in your school community.

Before selecting a project:

Assess and Envision Consider where you are starting from and what you might change.

- Think about how families are involved in the school now, and imagine what stronger, more positive family involvement might look like.

- What do you notice about the way things are now?

- How would you like things to be in the future?

- Do school families share that vision?

- Given the present level of family involvement, what might some comfortable initial events for families be?

Be purposeful Make sure you can explain what the school community will gain from involving families in the way(s) you have in mind.

- What are your goals?

- What results do you expect?

- Who will benefit and how?

Take stock Consider common knowledge and routines that will help family events go more smoothly. Make a plan for getting these things in place before the events take place.

- What do students, their families, and staff already know?

- What needs to be taught?

- To whom? By whom?

Once you have decided on a project:

Consider logistics Work out practical details beforehand.

- When and where will the event take place?

- What can you do to accommodate families' work schedules, transportation challenges, and child care needs?

- How will you get the word out about the event?

- How will visitors find their way around the school?

- Will they need seats?

- Will refreshments be provided?

- Where will they park?

- How will families be greeted as they enter the building?

- Will name tags be provided?

- What other details do you need to consider ahead of time?

Introduce the project Make sure everyone involved understands what is happening and why it's taking place.

- How will you introduce the project to school staff?

- How will families be invited?

- How will you introduce it to students?

Prepare students Build the specific skills that students need for the event. For this to succeed, what do people need to know how to do?

- What do students need to know how to do to navigate the event successfully?

- What do they need to think about ahead of time?

- When and how will the preparation take place?

Afterwards:

Evaluate Take time to reflect on how it went. Think about what could be improved, but be sure also to notice and celebrate what went well.

- Did it go as you expected?

- Were there any surprises?

- What went well?

- What could make this go better next time?

Remain purposeful As you think about next steps, consider your original reasons for doing this project.

- Did the event accomplish the purpose you originally set?

- Has your purpose changed?

- Is it time to set different goals?

The Responsive Classroom® Approach

Creating Safe, Challenging, and Joyful Elementary Classrooms and Schools

The *Responsive Classroom* approach is a way of teaching that emphasizes social, emotional, and academic growth in a strong and safe school community. Developed by classroom teachers in 1981 and continually refined to meet schools' needs, the approach consists of practical strategies for helping children build academic and social-emotional competencies day in and day out. In urban, suburban, and rural settings nationwide, educators using these strategies report increased student engagement and academic progress, along with fewer discipline problems.

Guiding Principles

The *Responsive Classroom* approach is informed by the work of educational theorists and the experiences of exemplary classroom teachers. Seven principles guide this approach:

- The social curriculum is as important as the academic curriculum.

- How children learn is as important as what they learn: Process and content go hand in hand.

- The greatest cognitive growth occurs through social interaction.

- To be successful academically and socially, children need a set of social skills: cooperation, assertion, responsibility, empathy, and self-control.

- Knowing the children we teach—individually, culturally, and developmentally— is as important as knowing the content we teach.

- Knowing the families of the children we teach and working with them as partners is essential to children's education.

- How the adults at school work together is as important as their individual competence: Lasting change begins with the adult community.

Classroom Practices

At the heart of the *Responsive Classroom* approach are ten classroom practices:

Morning Meeting—gathering as a whole class each morning to greet one another, share news, and warm up for the day ahead

Rule Creation—helping students create classroom rules that allow all class members to meet their learning goals

Interactive Modeling—teaching children to notice and internalize expected behaviors through a unique modeling technique

Positive Teacher Language—using words and tone to promote children's active learning and self-discipline

Logical Consequences—responding to misbehavior in a way that allows children to fix and learn from their mistakes while preserving their dignity

Guided Discovery—introducing materials using a format that encourages creativity and responsibility

Academic Choice—increasing student learning by allowing students teacher-structured choices in their work

Classroom Organization—setting up the physical room in ways that encourage independence, cooperation, and productivity

Working with Families—hearing families' insights and helping them understand the school's teaching approaches

Collaborative Problem Solving—using conferencing, role playing, and other strategies to engage students in problem solving

Schoolwide Implementation

After incorporating *Responsive Classroom* practices into classroom teaching, schools are often motivated to extend the principles of the approach to areas outside the classroom. They plan lunchroom and playground procedures, all-school events, and other aspects of whole-school life to ensure consistency in climate and expectations between the classroom and the larger school.

Schools implementing the *Responsive Classroom* approach schoolwide typically adopt the following practices:

Aligning policies and procedures with Responsive Classroom *philosophy*—making sure everything from the lunch routine to the discipline policy enhances the self-management skills that children are learning through the *Responsive Classroom* approach

Allocating resources to support Responsive Classroom *implementation*—using time, money, space, and personnel to support staff in learning and using the *Responsive Classroom* approach

Planning all-school activities to build a sense of community—giving all of the school's children and staff opportunities to learn about and from each other through activities such as all-school meetings, cross-age recess or lunch, buddy classrooms, and cross-age book clubs

Welcoming families and community members as partners—involving them in the children's education by maintaining two-way communication, inviting them to visit and volunteer, and offering family activities

Organizing the physical environment to set a tone of learning—making sure, for example, that schoolwide rules are posted prominently, displays emphasize student work, and all school spaces are welcoming, clean, and orderly

Visit our website—www.responsiveclassroom.org—to learn more about the *Responsive Classroom* approach

Professional Development Opportunities

- One-Day Workshops

- Week-Long Institutes

- Follow-Up Consultation

- Schoolwide Consultation

- *Responsive Classroom* Schools Conference

Publications

- Books and DVDs offering practical information for teachers and administrators

- Free quarterly newsletter with articles written by teachers for teachers

- Many free articles in our online archive

About Northeast Foundation for Children

Northeast Foundation for Children, Inc. (NEFC) is a nonprofit organization and the developer of the *Responsive Classroom* approach. NEFC was founded in 1981 by four public school educators who had a vision of bringing together social and academic learning throughout the school day. Today, NEFC has a staff of thirty who work at its Turners Falls, Massachusetts office developing resources, training, and materials to support successful and joyful learning communities. In addition, NEFC employs over 100 consulting teachers who work in the field helping teachers and schools throughout the country learn to use the *Responsive Classroom* approach.

NORTHEAST FOUNDATION FOR CHILDREN, INC.

85 Avenue A, Suite 204, P.O. Box 718, Turners Falls, MA 01376-0718

800-360-6332   FAX 877-206-3952

www.responsiveclassroom.org

Resources from Northeast Foundation for Children

99 Activities and Greetings: Great for Morning Meeting and Other Meetings, Too!
MELISSA CORREA-CONNOLLY. 2004. ■ A rich collection of group activities and greetings that give students practice in a wide range of social and academic skills.

Classroom Spaces that Work. MARLYNN CLAYTON WITH MARY BETH FORTON. 2001.
■ Learn to create a physical environment that is organized, welcoming, and well suited to the needs of students and teachers.

Creating a Safe and Friendly School: Lunchroom, Hallways, Playground and More.
2006. ■ Seventeen articles offer practical ideas for extending positive classroom climate to buses, hallways, lunchrooms, special area classrooms, playgrounds, and bathrooms.

Familiar Ground: Traditions that Build School Community. LIBBY WOODFIN.1998.
■ Describes traditions and ceremonies that build a sense of school community at one K–8 school.

The First Six Weeks of School. PAULA DENTON AND ROXANN KRIETE. 2000. ■ Build a solid foundation during the first weeks of school, and you'll find it pays off in more learning and fewer problem behaviors throughout the year.

Kids Taking Action: Community Service Learning Projects, K–8. PAMELA ROBERTS. 2002.
■ Profiles eighteen hands-on, kid-friendly community service learning projects from classrooms across the country.

Learning Through Academic Choice. PAULA DENTON. 2005. ■ Learn step-by-step how to use Academic Choice, a powerful teaching tool that increases students' motivation and academic skills.

The Morning Meeting Book. ROXANN KRIETE WITH CONTRIBUTIONS BY LYNN BECHTEL. 2002.
■ A guidebook for using Morning Meeting, a simple and powerful teaching tool for building community, increasing student investment, and improving academic and social skills.

Morning Meeting Messages: 180 Sample Charts from Three Classrooms.
ROSALEA FISHER, ERIC HENRY, AND DEBORAH PORTER. 2006. ■ Daily charts collected from a K–1, 3rd, and 5th grade classroom annotated to show how a welcoming, well crafted morning message can help students learn at their best throughout the day.

Parents and Teachers Working Together. CAROL DAVIS AND ALICE YANG. 2005.
■ Manageable ways to build positive relationships with parents and work with them to support their children's learning all year long.

The Power of Our Words: Teacher Language that Helps Children Learn. PAULA DENTON.
2007. ■ Learn to use language more skillfully, building a classroom where students feel safe, respected, appreciated, and excited about learning.

Rules in School. KATHRYN BRADY, MARY BETH FORTON, DEBORAH PORTER, AND CHIP WOOD.
2003. ■ Learn an approach to discipline that gets students invested in creating and living by classroom rules.

Teaching Children to Care: Classroom Management for Ethical and Academic Growth, K–8. RUTH SIDNEY CHARNEY. 2002. ■ A comprehensive guide on classroom management that will help you turn your vision of respectful, friendly, academically rigorous classrooms into reality.

Time to Teach, Time to Learn: Changing the Pace of School. CHIP WOOD. 1999.
■ Administrative and teaching strategies that make more time for reflection, dialogue, rigorous academics, and meaningful social interaction.

Yardsticks: Children in the Classroom Ages 4-14 (3rd ed.) CHIP WOOD. 2007. ■ Clear, concise information about children's development and needs at each age, four through fourteen.

Karen L. Casto began her teaching career in 1972 and has taught in middle school, high school, and college. She was a middle and high school administrator before becoming principal of Penn Valley Elementary School in Levittown, Pennsylvania and serving in that role for nine years. She is currently a consulting administrator for Northeast Foundation for Children. Karen has a BA from Muhlenberg College, an MEd from Temple University, and an EdD from Lehigh University.

Jennifer R. Audley has experience as a classroom teacher at the elementary, middle, and high school levels. She joined the staff of Northeast Foundation for Children in 2005, bringing experience as a writer, researcher, editor, and educational consultant. She has a BA from Vassar College and an EdM from Harvard Graduate School of Education.